POINTS IN TIME

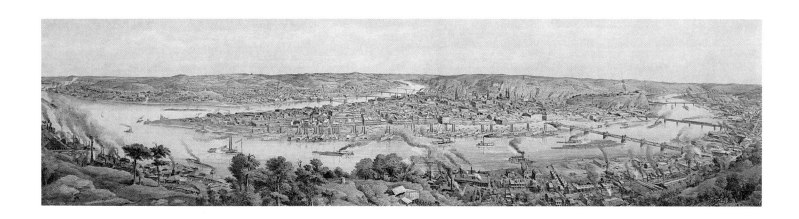

"Pittsburgh, Allegheny & Birmingham 1871"
by Otto Krebs
Chromo-lithograph on wove paper
54.9 cm x 115.4 cm
Historical Society of Western Pennsylvania Museum Collection

POINTS IN TIME:
Building a Life in Western Pennsylvania

Paul Roberts, Editor

A Companion to the Historical Society of Western Pennsylvania Exhibition
"Points in Time: Building a Life in Western Pennsylvania, 1750 - Today"
The Senator John Heinz Pittsburgh Regional History Center

Opening April 1996

Historical Society of Western Pennsylvania
Pittsburgh, Pennsylvania
1996

Copyright © 1996 by Historical Society of Western Pennsylvania
1212 Smallman Street
Pittsburgh, Pennsylvania 15222-4200
412/454-6000
All rights reserved. Manufactured in the United States of America.
First Edition.

ISBN 0-936340-00-2

"Pittsburgh, The Point from
 Mt. Washington"
by Thornton Oakley, 1914
Charcoal and watercolor wash on paper
28.25 x 15.65inches
Historical Society of Western Pennsylvania
Museum Collection, Gift of the artist

Background photograph by Nina Margiotta

Contents

Acknowledgements i
By William W. Keyes, Museum Director

Preface, History as an Object Lesson iv
By Paul Roberts, Editor

Introduction, History as Conversation vi
By Thomas J. Schlereth, University of Notre Dame

Chapter 1, A Contested Land, 1750-1820 1
Essay & Captions by Gary Pollock

Chapter 2, City on the Move, 1815-1875 17
Essay & Captions by Anne Madarasz

Chapter 3, The Industrial City, 1870-1930 35
Essay by Philip Scranton & Anizia Karmazyn-Olijar; Captions by Karmazyn-Olijar

Chapter 4, The Hill: A City Neighborhood, 1900-1940 65
Essay & Captions by Teresa Lynne Riesmeyer

Chapter 5, Moving to the Suburbs, 1945-1965 87
Essay & Captions by Gregory W. Smith

Chapter 6, After the Renaissance, 1965-1995 103
Essay by Michelle C.Fanzo & Captions by Gregory W. Smith

Illustration Credits 122

Acknowledgements

By William W. Keyes, Museum Director

In an exhibition project of six years' duration, with the ambitious scope of "Points In Time," dozens of people contribute in time, sweat, and spirit. Taking spirit first, I want to recognize the guiding role of Executive Director John A. Herbst, whose unflinching vision has been a constant beacon over the past 10 years. The Historical Society's Board of Trustees, too, have weathered the many storms that threatened our journey. Of particular help were David McCullough, Steven Graffam, William C. King, Van Beck Hall, and Robert Barensfeld.

Some of the principal early contributors to the exhibition did not stay on to participate in this catalog. Nonetheless, they charted the course or, at least, targeted some of its ultimate destinations. They are Bart A. Roselli, Thomas D. Carroll, and Susan Showalter.

Two people have made contributions beyond all reasonable expectations. Susan Page Tillet, who has served as principal exhibit consultant for the final year, brought her considerable experience, lightning insights and unflagging good cheer. Thomas

J. Schelereth, who wrote the introduction for this catalog and reviewed all exhibit scripts, gave generously of his time and talent from the earliest days of exhibit development through to final script polishing.

Much of the success of the exhibition is due to the creative work of Vincent Ciulla Design of New York. The firm's perseverance and imagination made the ideas real. Vincent Ciulla, Julie Ciulla, and Jennifer Murphy, with John Carson, fashioned an experience, not just an exhibit.

Through the generous support of the National Endowment for the Humanities, distinguished scholars, curators, and museum professionals from around the country met with HSWP staff to review outlines, exhibit scripts and the essays in this catalog. The NEH grant funded several lively round table reviews with Wendy Aibel-weiss, Kenneth L. Ames, Linda Rosenzweig, Betty Sharp, Margaret Spratt, Joe W. Trotter, and Michael Wallace.

Historians at the University of Pittsburgh, Carnegie Mellon University and Duquesne University assisted with informed

i

reviews of exhibit scripts and catalog essays. Always at the ready were Laurence Glasco, Maurine Greenwald, Van Beck Hall, Edward K. Muller, Joel Tarr and Michael Wallace. Pittsburgh native Philip Scranton of the Hagley Institute also qualifies as ever-ready for his review of labels and his catalog essay contribution.

Specialists in other fields offered unequaled assistance on the exhibit: Frank C. Bolden, Edna Mackenzie and Charles "Teenie" Harris for their work on the *Pittsburgh Courier* section; C. Hax McCullough for the French and Indian War section; and Claudia Lamm Wood, Jeff MacGregor and Karen Cooper Bowden for exhibit script editing.

The success of the voyage has been due to the stamina, courage, growth, and spirit of the staff at the Historical Society. The seminal participation of Carolyn Sutcher Schumacher, Ann A. Fortescue, Don C. Traub, and Ellen Rosenthal launched this exhibition. The curators of the exhibit, Anizia Karmazyn-Olijar, Anne Madarasz, Gary Pollock and Greg Smith, teased from our collections a masterful story of the region. Each of them also is represented in this catalog. Teresa Riesmeyer, project archivist and catalog essayist, pursued the hundreds of images for the exhibit and the catalog with the relentlessness of Ahab, assisted by Karen Hockenson. Project Historian Elizabeth Watkins, a latecomer to the project, has shepherded the labels through their evolution to finished copy and rescued several drifting sections.

Paul Roberts, the editor of this volume, made strategic improvements in the catalog's content, secured numerous images not found in the exhibition and, with the help of Marilyn Erwin and Brian A. Butko, burnished the prose into an exhibit catalog that stands on its own as a book as well. Kathleen Wendell and the registration staff have preserved and presented the collections of the Historical Society with professional zeal and a generous spirit, including Linda Pelan, William Kinderland and Jennifer Smith. Sig Tragard brought his eternal optimism and exhibit experience that made the exhibit fabrication outstanding. With Gordon Macshane II as exhibit construction manager, they have turned the text, artifacts and images into a truly exciting experience. Administrative assistant Mark Tabbert kept the ship on course; without him we would surely would have run aground. We also had the specialized help of Catherine Cerrone, Lynne Conner, R. Craig Koedel, Patricia Pugh Mitchell, Lauren Uhl and Tracy Coffin Walther, whose expertise saved us from looming disaster. And last but not least, three dedicated people untiringly searched and found, checked and rechecked: Joan Kimmel, Joan Kubancek, and Chrisoula Randas-Perdziola. The staff was backed up by the patient and generous work of volunteers and interns Johanna Cormier, Heather J. Erskine, Michael Jula, Mark Kelly, Hilary Krueger, Jennifer L. Lapp, Rebecca Pilliteri, and Kimberly Root.

Most of the objects and material for illustrations used in this project came from the archival, library and museum collections of the Historical Society of Western Pennsylvania. Curators and archivists at libraries, museums and private collections in the United States and abroad also have loaned artifacts and images that appear in the exhibit and in this catalog. Their kind assistance has allowed us to include the best materials available, much previously unknown to the public. Our special thanks goes to Atwater-Kent Museum, A.P./Widewide Photos, Bethel A.M.E. Church, British Library Department of Manuscripts, Carnegie Library of Pittsburgh, Carnegie Mellon University's Hunt Library, the Carnegie Museum of Art, Clark America, Croatian Fraternal Union of America, Dawes Library at Marietta College, Eat'n Park, International Museum of Photography at George Eastman House, the Frick Art and Historical Center, Hagley Museum and Library, Harvard University's Carpenter Center for the Arts, Historical Society of Pennsylvania, Jewish Community Center of Pittsburgh, Johnstown Area Heritage Association, Library of Congress, Lincoln University's Langston Hughes Memorial Library, Meadowcroft Museum of Rural Life, Mellon Bank, Metropolitan Museum of Art, Milwaukee Public Museum, Motion Picture Academy, Multi-Cultural Center of Ontario, National Archives, National Baseball Hall of Fame and Museum, Inc., Newberry Library, the New-York Historical Society, Patch/Work Voices Project (Pennsylvania State University—Fayette Campus), Roman Catholic Diocese of Pittsburgh, Pennsylvania State University Archives, Saints Peter & Paul Ukrainian Orthodox Greek Catholic Church, *Pittsburgh Courier* Photographic Archives, *Pittsburgh Post-Gazette*, Seneca-Iroquois National Museum, *Sports Illustrated-*Time Life, State Museum of Pennsylvania, Smithsonian National Museum of American History, University of Pittsburgh's Archives of Industrial Society, University of Pittsburgh Artificial Heart Program, Virginia Historical Society, Washington & Jefferson College Historical Collections, Wheaton Village Museum of American Glass, Winterthur Museum, YWCA National Board Archives.

In addition to the National Endowment for the Humanities, support was provided by The Ellwood Group, Inc. for the *Industrial Section*; Blue Cross of Western Pennsylvania; the Hospital Council of Western Pennsylvania; Chevron, Inc. for *Gulf Oil materials*; Eat'n Park Restaurants, Inc. for *Car Culture*; Martha Mack Lewis for the *Courtyard*; T. Bruce Dickson, Mrs. Charles Fleischmann III, and Fredrick J. Stevenson, Jr, *Thaw Family Section*; Leon Falk Family Trust for *Costumes*; Pennsylvania Historical and Museum Commission; Pittsburgh Coal Mining Institute of America, and the Society of Mining Engineers, Pittsburgh Section for *Mining History*; SmithKline Beecham Foundation for *Access for People with Disabilities*, and Mr. and Mrs. John N. Tarr for *Log House*.

There are also those who contributed by kind encouragement, saintly patience, and generous indulgence: the families, friends and loved ones of the staff and consultants.

I also want to name the late Professor David C. Huntington, my mentor at the University of Michigan, who knew how to see the beauty and subtlety of artifacts and how to convey a love of history.

Preface

History as an Object Lesson

By Paul Roberts, Editor

What you hold in your hands is a guide to an exhibition at a new urban history museum, the Senator John Heinz Pittsburgh Regional History Center. It is also more than a guide. This is the place where those who did the research and collected the artifacts for the exhibition extend their analyses of the region's history beyond the confines of the History Center's galleries.

When the exhibition, "Points in Time: Building a Life in Western Pennsylvania, 1750-Today," began to take shape at the Historical Society, more than five years ago, a central concern was where to begin the historical narrative and where to end it. It was decided that visitors would want to see a "full story," beginning in the era of Pittsburgh's founding and ending in the modern day. We were aware that with such a broad sweep, covering more than 200 years, many important events and decades in the region's past would recieve little or no mention. We also knew that several centuries of civilization by Native Americans, before white Europeans claimed the land in the 17th century, would receive practically

no attention. Exhibitions in coming years at the History Center will address many of the gaps in the "Points in Time" permanent exhibition.

For this book, two nationally recognized authorities on museumship (Thomas Schlereth of the University of Notre Dame and Philip Scranton from the Hagley Museum and Library) bolstered the work of our own staff. And, to bring the time covered by these essays to the present, we turned to Michelle Fanzo, a free-lance journalist who specializes in writing about Pittsburgh's history and economy. We felt that the training and practices of a historian or a staff curator did not prepare either very well for assessing the events of the 1980s in Pittsburgh, especially the tremendous economic changes.

Tom Schlereth, in the introduction which follows this preface, observes that people leave their personal and communal histories in written and spoken narratives — in stories. This is a simple but highly useful concept for all who study and try to understand the past. It serves equally well the professional historian in schools, colleges and universities, the curator at museums and historic sites, and individuals who pursue an interest in history after the regular work day is over. That in our stories we leave our history is, in part, what motivates even random acts of historical interest, such as stopping on the side of the road to read an historical marker.

Our narratives are not only what humans have said or written, however. There are also the more silent types. A bone carving, a craftsman's cabinet, a corporate president's chair, a coal miner's tool, and a debutante's opera cloak — they all tell a story.

Our families can hold some of the objects and relate some of the stories, but the narratives will necessarily be highly personal. That's where museums come in: they save the things of the past on a grander scale, to tell the stories of our peoples' shared history. Museums also incorporate the work of professional historians, making available specialized knowledge to the general public. When museum programs, exhibitions, and publications work well, crossing this unique knowledge bridge is an educational and entertaining experience.

Because people most often go to a history museum to see things, museum professionals depend on objects in the stories we tell. Those responsible for this book and exhibition certainly relied as well on words, from books and archival documents, but the museum approach emphasizes artifacts.

"Material culture" is an academic name for these things left behind; Schlereth defines the term "as the vast universe of objects made and used by humankind to cope with the physical world, to facilitate social intercourse, to delight our fancy, and to create symbols of meaning." Some objects identified as Western Pennsylvania examples of material culture, found in this book and in the exhibition, include: David Shaw's fowling rifle (p. 6); George Morgan's silk waistcoat (p. 7); Mary Mejer's lace engagement cap (p. 45); the Joe Magarac model (p. 108).

By seeing these and other artifacts in the exhibition, one can make his or her own interpretations of use and meaning; those interpretations then can be weighed with others' written or spoken words about such objects. Past human activity, notes Schlereth, receives a novel degree of permanency and immediacy in material culture.

Until now, interpretations of the history of Pittsburgh and its region went on primarily in academic institutions, where the use of archival records — not objects and photographs — is emphasized. Large-scale collecting of three-dimensional artifacts by a professional history organization devoted to public exhibitions, however, is a relatively recent activity in Pittsburgh; only in the last decade has the Historical Society of Western Pennsylvania had this mission and been especially active. The "Points in Time" exhibition and catalog are the fruits of that effort, and they also stand as the first comprehensive presentation of Pittsburgh history to be attempted.

Pittsburgh has a unique past as a river port that helped transform the interior of the continent and, later, as an industrial workshop with few rivals. Many aspects of its past are representative of America's history, as well as unique. This is what we hope to relate in this communal story that concentrates on the region's largest city. Any generalization will slight the details, but the story told on a grand scale with objects, words, and pictures is fascinating. We feel certain it will enlighten and entertain.

Introduction

History as Conversation

By Thomas J. Schlereth, University of Notre Dame

"In a certain sense," wrote British author Thomas Carlyle, "all men are historians. Most speak only to narrate." In our narratives — written, spoken, crafted — we leave our histories. These histories are both personal and communal stories. They also can be thought of as conversations.

This collection of essays, and the museum exhibition it accompanies, recognizes the multiplicity of historical evidence that survives from the past and the multitude of historical narratives that can be told from such material. Both emphasize physical, visual, tactile artifacts, arguing that as important as the ideas are that Western Pennsylvanians wrote down, so too are the innumerable things they left behind.

The Essayists' City and Region

What common ground do the authors share in their discussions of Pittsburgh and Western Pennsylvania history? While they address most of the city's major historical events (for example, the nationwide Railroad Strike of 1877) and note many of its important figures (for example, Mayor David Lawrence), their overall emphasis is not on the area's most dramatic episodes or its most famous (or infamous) citizens. Readers will meet well-known Pittsburghers such as Edward Braddock, Andrew Carnegie, Henry Frick, and Andrew Mellon; but they will also encounter many others less familiar: Colonel George Morgan, a Revolutionary War officer stationed at Fort Pitt; banker and real estate promoter John Thaw, who managed the finances of the Monongahela Bridge Company prior to the Panic of 1837; Mikolai Koval, Greek immigrant worker, killed May 9, 1916 in a mill accident in Johnstown; African American business entrepreneur Gus Greenlee, who owned the Crawford Grill on Wylie Avenue and the Pittsburgh Crawfords baseball team; and Ann McCastland, a factory worker at the Westinghouse plant during World War II. As we learn the stories of these people's pasts, one thinks of Warrick who, in Shakespeare's Henry IV, reminds us that: "There is a history in all men's lives."

The significance of place — be it regional, urban, neighborhood, suburban — overlaps all of our authors' interpretations. The numerous maps, city plans, bird's-eye views, lithographs, and aerial photographs in this book (and throughout the exhibition) attest to the enormous importance of topography and geography in shaping Western Pennsylvania and Pittsburgh history. A quick review of the graphics found at the end of each essay will provide readers with a visual sequence of the physical evolution of the region and city from 1805 to 1995.

In the book's first essay, **Gary Pollock**, assistant curator at the Historical Society, traces the region's earliest occupation by Europeans. His emphasis is on the area's three major watercourses and how Pittsburgh's location at their convergence enabled it to best other river towns and would-be urban rivals such as Uniontown, Brownsville and Washington for economic supremacy. Geopolitics and local politics both figure significantly in 18th-century military struggles over Fort Duquesne and Fort Pitt, and in the contest among European powers and their Native American allies for the North American continent. Pollock's essay also shows how being a military base assured the governmental commerce that helped fuel Pittsburgh's economic ascendancy — a symbiotic relationship evident again during the Civil War and World War I and II.

Anne Madarasz, a project curator at the Historical Society, addresses antebellum Pittsburgh during its first commercial boom. Glass production, which expands dramatically during the 19th century, gets its proper treatment. So do the implications of the Western Pennsylvania population explosion; its new economic enterprises (textiles, natural gas); and its most devastating urban calamity to date: the Great Fire of 1845.

Madarasz prompts us to think comparatively when doing urban history — for example, with Cincinnati and St. Louis, which both surpassed Pittsburgh in total population by 1850. How, in turn, might Pittsburgh's history also be compared to that of other Ohio river towns such as Louisville? What would we learn by contrasting it with the growth of Cleveland and Chicago, two of its industrial rivals? How has Pittsburgh, over its long history, defined itself vis-a-vis Harrisburg, Pennsylvania's capital since 1812, or Philadelphia, the state's largest metropolis since colonial times?

Birmingham and Allegheny City, two other urban communities that grew up alongside the Point, are also discussed in Chapter 2. Allegheny City, a North Side community of small businesses and breweries, figured as an early bedroom suburb for some downtown workers. Suburbanization, a movement many people usually associate only with 20th-century demographic patterns, is well underway in Pittsburgh by the 1850s, suggests Madarasz, with new residential developments in Sewickley and the East End.

Philip Scranton, director of the Center for the History of Business, Technology, and Society at the Hagley Museum and Library in Wilmington, Delaware, with the assistance of HSWP Curator **Anizia Karmazyn-Olijar**, takes on the period of Western Pennsylvania's past that American history texts always include — the era of the Homestead strike of 1892, the attempted assassination of capitalist H. C. Frick by anarchist Alexander Berkman and the emergence of U.S. Steel as one of the nation's corporate giants. In their review of these events, Scranton and Karmazyn-Olijar also alert us to other historical trends. Their tracking of changes in the making of steel, for example, gives us a succinct chapter in the history of technology; explaining how it (and other metal products of the region) was sold via a diversified market acts as a summary of Western Pennsylvania's economic history. Here we also have an accounting of Pittsburgh's emergence as a significant financial center whose banks — for example, those of the Mellon family — funded numerous industrial enterprises throughout the region.

To run corporations such as U.S. Steel, Westinghouse Electric or Gulf Oil required a paper empire manned by a workforce of clerical and office personnel whose historical role has been obscured by Pittsburgh's traditional blue-collar image. As early as 1910, however, 9.8 per cent of the city's jobs were white-collar, a percentage that has increased throughout the 20th century in Pittsburgh.

Urban historians sometimes write of cities as the result of theoretical processes (for example, urbanization) or as abstract geographical aggregates (for example, Metropolitan Population Areas). Urban residents, however, know different. To many of them, such generalizations are only partially useful when describing city life. Instead, the history of neighborhoods — parts not the whole — reveal much of a city's character, diversity, and distinctiveness.

Teresa Riesmeyer, who is the project archivist for the exhibition, explores this idea by devoting Chapter 4 to a Pittsburgh neighborhood — one known since the 1840s as simply "the Hill." There are perhaps 90 identifiable neighborhoods in the city, but the Hill was chosen because it is a residential and commercial community with a 150-year history and because people from two dozen of the city's ethnic and racial groups have called it home — the largest in number being Scots-Irish and Germans in the late 19th century, followed by Jews and African Americans in the 20th century. The area also serves as a case study for understanding the problematical impact of federal urban renewal policies and the municipal urban planning that produced Pittsburgh's Renaissance I but in the process also displaced 2,000 families and 416 businesses from the Hill neighborhood.

In her analysis of this single space, Riesmeyer chronicles several typically urban spaces — settlement houses, the YWCA and YMCA, public baths, and jazz clubs. Wylie Avenue, a thoroughfare running the length of the Hill District and a street comparable to Auburn Avenue in Atlanta or Beale Street in Memphis, served the African American community (75 percent of the neighborhood's population by 1950) as the Hill's commercial and cultural spine.

In the late 19th century, many white residents departed the Hill for communities like Oakland and Shadyside. This suburban outmigration, as **Gregory W. Smith**, former assistant curator, shows in Chapter 5, has numerous parallels in the various forms of

Pittsburgh's Point, 1995
by Nina Margiotta

suburbia to which Pittsburghers have moved throughout the twentieth century. The geographical direction of this movement (physically as well as economically) can be roughly monitored by its chronological sequence: to East End suburbs first, then the South Hills, followed by the North Hills.

Smith singles out two of the area's suburbs — West Mifflin (a blue-collar industrial suburb) and Pleasant Hills (a white-collar commuter suburb) —to characterize post-WWII residential patterns. In the historical development of West Mifflin, we encounter a suburban settlement form that has frequently encircled Pittsburgh. Some urban historians have labeled these communities as industrial suburbs; others call them industrial towns. Whatever the nomenclature, they have been prolific on the Western Pennsylvania landscape; there is one for almost every letter of the alphabet: Aliquippa, Braddock, Clairton, Duquesne, East Pittsburgh.

Our final essayist, **Michelle C. Fanzo**, a journalist who specializes in modern Pittsburgh's economic conditions, argues in her appraisal of the region since 1965 that the past three decades are best explained by demographics and economics. While previous essayists could tally the continuing growth of the area's population, her statistics are the opposite — the city of Pittsburgh, for example, has lost 45 percent of its citizens since 1950. The remaining population has, compared with other American cities, fewer young people and more retirees. Steel manufacturing jobs, once the key economic indicator for the region, dropped from 150,000 in the 1950s to 20,000 by the 1990s. In her account of Big Steel's decline, Fanzo introduces us to Charlie McCollester, a shop steward at Union Switch and Signal. At the initial meeting of the Tri-State Conference on Steel in 1979, McCollester, in a gesture of high drama and in a powerful use of material culture, threw a century-old piece of steel rail from the Edgar Thomson Works into the middle of the meeting room. "Someday," announced McCollester prophetically, "we are going to have to go to a museum to see this, because there won't be any steel left in the Mon Valley."

The Exhibition's City and Region

Interpreting the 250-year history of the 10 generations of people who have lived within the present 55 square miles of Pittsburgh's city limits, or the 727 square miles of Allegheny County, or the 62,000 square miles of Western Pennsylvania, is an enormous undertaking. No one has ever done it. In creating their long-term exhibition of the history of Pittsburgh and its region, the team of historians, curators, consultants, and designers who researched and fabricated "Points in Time" have aspired to be as geographically and chronologically comprehensive as possible. They were able to house their urban history presentation in an urban artifact (the Chautauqua Lake Ice Company, built in 1898) which survives in one of the city's historic urban areas (the Strip District). Site and structure are used as mini-exhibits, for they encapsulate themes in the area's economic, industrial, and consumer history.

The Chautauqua Ice House and the Strip District — like the History Center within them — are places. As three-dimensional material culture, they quickly prompt a sense of the human activity that has taken place in space past as well as time past. Throughout the "Points in Time" exhibition (the Point being one of Pittsburgh's most enduring iconical spaces), place is frequently used to situate the area's history. This is not surprising in a region with place-names such as Panther Hollow, Neville's Island, Sawmill Run, Squirrel Hill, Mount Troy, Coal Bluff, McKees Rocks, and Millvale. The exhibition itself could be summarized by generic places such as the wharf, the hill, the neighborhood, the valley, the triangle, the mill, the suburb, the home.

Cities like Pittsburgh are humankind's largest collective assemblages of art and artifice, of culture and material culture. They are palimpsests of civil, economic, transportation, and social history as well as above-ground archaeological sites containing enormous collections of sensory, olfactory, and auditory historical evidence. In brief, cities (and regions on a larger scale) are gigantic outdoor museums — if we know how to look at them. Urban history museums help us do this. For example, at the Pittsburgh Regional History Center, we learn how to decipher fire-insurance maps, work with city directories, and interpret city planning proposals. We also learn that just as there are many portals to a city and many avenues into its history, the "Points in Time" exhibition has several points of entry into the region's past. From the central plaza, we can choose to enter any of three sites: a 1780 log cabin, a 1910 steelworker's house, or a 1950s suburban home. History is where we start it.

Homeplaces, material culture common to us all, are commonly where many of us start our histories. Appropriately, therefore, the exhibition gives special priority to the history of the region's homeplaces. It does so in several formats: in plans (Fort Pitt barracks; King Place tract), in models (John Thaw house; Swift Homes); in photographs (The Pittsburgh Survey); and in full-scale replications (frontier cabin, immigrant home, suburban residence). Within this residential triptych stands the two-story steelworker's house and courtyard, dramatizing both the exhibition's spatial center and its main interpretative focus: work and home.

Domestic artifacts are any culture's most abundant material culture. While seemingly only the assorted rummage of everyday life, the objects of home and household provide insight into human aspiration and ingenuity, accomplishment and identity. Take, for example, the kerosene lamp in the exhibition's fourth section. While it was a utilitarian, portable light source for many immigrant residents of the Hill neighborhood, it could also take on a more profound function, serving as this one did, to illuminate the celebration of the Seder for a Jewish family in the early 20th century.

A peoples' past, evident in their homeplaces, can also be found in community spaces. The exhibition emphasizes urban spaces — some originating in the region (John B. Harris's 1905 nickelodeons in McKeesport and Pittsburgh), others generic to modern urban history (department stores such as Boggs and Buhl and social settlements such as the Irene Kaufman house). Urban play places like Forbes Field, Schenley Park, and Kennywood Park are likewise featured.

Workplaces and workers constitute a second major focus of "Points in Time." Traditional occupations — the military, farming, artisanry, business, housewifery, mining, domestic service — receive their due. Work sites new to the last two centuries are also examined: department stores, coal company towns, corporate offices, garment sweatshops, and real estate agencies.

Historical evidence like the Fort Pitt daybook, city directories, cigar presses, a report card from Connelly Trade School, personalized hard hats, the uniform of a department store employee, the heat suit of a steel worker, and a factory danger sign in five languages, document both the work life and the work ethic that characterize much of the city's history. Photography also reveals the region's labor force at work (the captivating albums of Lyon, Shorb Company in Birmingham); at home (company house #45 in Whitsett); and at play (picnics at Camp Horne and Kennywood); and out of work (Lockwood Hoehl's photographs of the Duquesne Steel Works).

The "Points in Time" exhibition recognizes that workers are people — an important fact that macro-economists, efficiency experts, and even some labor historians sometimes forget. Its workplaces are abundantly peopled. You will meet: military agent James O'Hara; businessman Michael Allen; social worker Anna B. Heldman, businesswoman Virginia Proctor. Also Dr. Martin Delany, editor of *The Mystery*, the first African American newspaper west of the Alleghenies; Modelona Osthoff Lukey, an early 19th-century silversmith's wife; and Charles "Teenie" Harris, a self-taught photographer for the *Pittsburgh Courier*. Pittsburghers as special groups — Native Americans, women, and minorities — also receive attention, perhaps more on the exhibition's floor than in this publication's pages.

In that exhibition space, Western Pennsylvanians narrate their histories in various ways. First, in a 10-minute introductory video in the exhibition's orientation theater; then through three interactive, audio-equipped kiosks that connect the six sections of the exhibition. Throughout the exhibition one will read or hear excerpts from letters, diaries, personal journals and conversations.

History as a Conversation

History as conversation was the metaphor I used to introduce both this book and the exhibition, "Points in Time." It is not a novel concept. A fellow historian, the late Douglass Adair, wrote: "History is a conversation about the past in the present for the future."

I see history's discourse about Pittsburgh and its region as an ongoing conversation, some of whose voices are found in this volume and still more are heard in the exhibition. In researching and writing the essays that follow, the authors have, in one sense, interrogated men and women from Western Pennsylvania's past. Together with the responses they heard from these first-hand participants, they have also listened to other historians, past and present, who continued the conversation.

Similarly, and simultaneously, curators, librarians, consultants, archivists, and exhibit designers working at the HSWP over the past five years have been carrying on their own conversation — one whose subject has been how best they might articulate, with words and things, what life was like in Western Pennsylvania in the period 1750-1990.

With this book's publication and the exhibition's opening, still others will join the discussion. Readers and visitors will add their voices to the conversation as they become involved with the words and things that survive from the region's past; as they test the ideas of those who have developed a historical interpretation of the city and its region in this book and exhibition; and, as they converse with each other about what all this might mean for the people who live and work in Pittsburgh and Western Pennsylvania today and for their children tomorrow. History as Conversation — about the past, in the present, for the future.

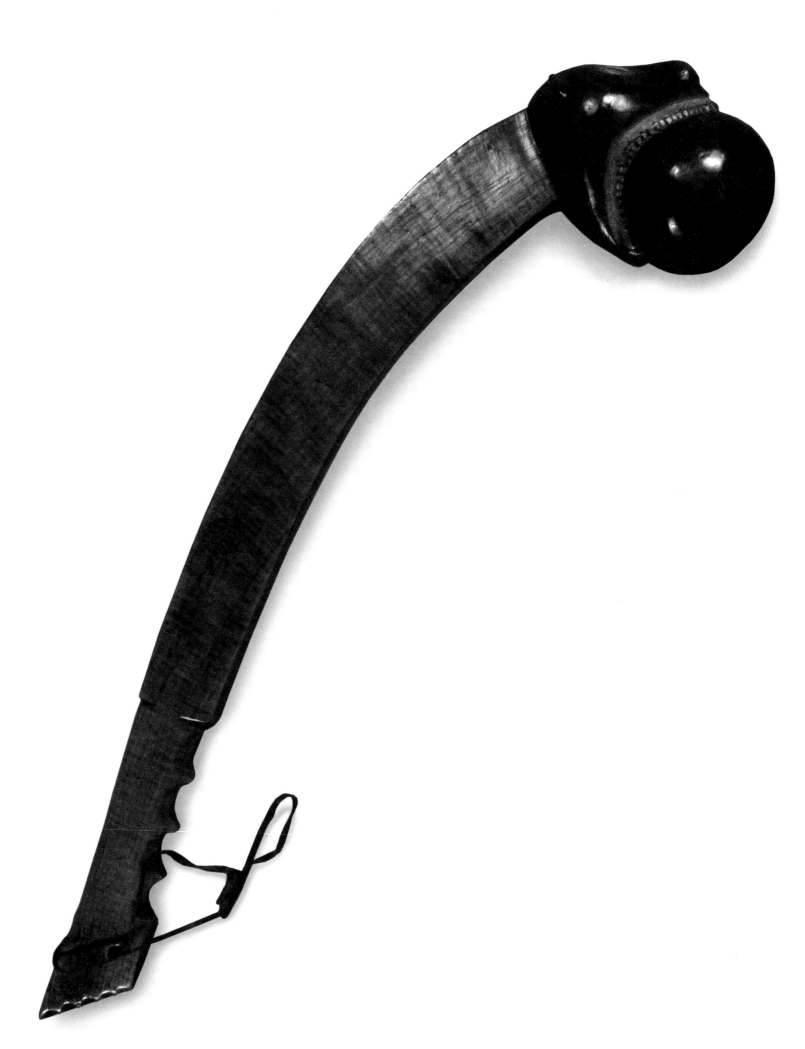

CHAPTER I

A Contested Land

1745-1820

Essay & Captions by Gary Pollock

Western Pennsylvania, between 1745 and 1820, developed rapidly from what Europeans considered a remote, unsettled frontier – a homeland for a vast complex of native cultures – into a well-established society with Pittsburgh, a bustling town called the "Gateway to the West," at its center. The strategic location of the region also included parts of present-day Ohio, Maryland, New York, and West Virginia. Drawn into the complicated military conflict were Native Americans, French, British, and colonial Americans from several colonies besides Pennsylvania, while settlers, speculators, artisans, and traders with no strict allegiances also took part. After winning the imperial contest for the land, the British, and later the Americans, attempted to protect their interests by building forts throughout the area. Settlement soon followed.

Many early settlers worked the land, but the region's economy quickly moved beyond farming. Work in the developing industries and towns brought together artisans, professionals, traders and laborers. Although other towns in the vicinity briefly competed with Pittsburgh in size and prestige, the city named for British Prime

Ball head club, Iroquois (early 19th century)
The years surrounding Pittsburgh's founding were ones of conflict in Eastern America among warring nations and their Native American allies. The wooden ball head club, or *gajewa*, was the favorite weapon of Iroquois warriors because of its sacred character derived from association with hand-to-hand combat. Early artifacts from Native American society in the East are rare; the general relationship between whites and Indians was peaceful and commercial; warfare was infrequent.

Minister William Pitt emerged, with its industry and prominent position on three rivers, as the city to which others nearby were compared to and as the area's economic powerhouse.

The years between 1745 and 1760 were ones of diplomatic negotiations and bitter confrontation over control of Western Pennsylvania's land and resources. Delaware, Shawnee, Seneca, Fox, and Wyandot Indians migrated to the area either to escape disease, famine, or colonial expansion in their homelands, or to find independence. British Americans had designs to occupy and settle the land. French and Canadian traders, who did not want settlements, tried to stop the British.

Military campaigns helped lay an economic foundation for the region. In 1759, the British built Fort Pitt on the abandoned ruins of the French Fort Duquesne at the forks of the Ohio River. Military garrisons needed provisions, so forts quickly developed their own economies. Officers used a variety of measures to acquire needed supplies. Faced with shortages and poor roads, many military leaders turned to Indians for food. When the Indians began to migrate further west in the 1770s, the military gradually relied more upon white settlements for supplies. American soldiers faced similar constraints after the British were driven out. During the American Revolution, for example, Fort Pitt's Col. George Morgan, rather than endure the costly and time-consuming process of procuring military goods from eastern commissary agents, contracted with local millers and farmers to provide flour, bacon, and beef.

The needs for provisions increased in the 1780s, when the U.S. government expanded its authority north and west of Pennsylvania into the area known then as the Northwest Territory. There were approximately 800 men stationed throughout the territory in the 1780s, and this number increased in the 1790s. Again, the military turned to local residents to supply military goods. One military agent, James O'Hara, contracted with local farmers and millers to supply flour, beef, and bacon, while his boatman transported these goods west.

Although militarily occupied, Western Pennsylvania was initially set aside for Native Americans. The region was officially closed to white settlement. But individuals crossed the Appalachian Mountains and illegally "squatted" on the land. In 1768, the lands were officially opened, and settlers streamed into a land described by Joshua Gilpin as "entirely composed of hills of every size mingled with each other – these are nei-

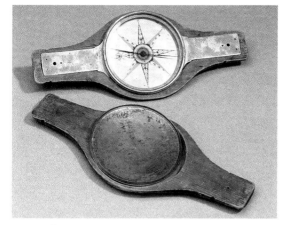

Circumferentor

Wherever frontiersman Christopher Gist went with the circumferentor compass (c. 1796), he created a stir among native inhabitants. Accurate measurements were needed for the maps that would lead more whites into the region. "It was dangerous," Gist learned, "to let a Compass be seen about the Indians." He came in 1750 unofficially to survey land for the Ohio Company of Virginia, but his larger purpose was to set up a council between the Indians and Virginia colonial authorities.

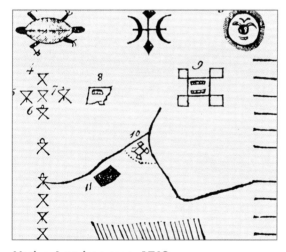

Native American map, 1762

Wingenund, a Munsee Indian prophet, depicted on sugar maple bark the domain of Native Americans that whites called the Ohio Country. It also depicts the British occupation. The three lines in the center represent the Allegheny, Monongahela, and Ohio rivers. At their junction is Fort Pitt, and the black, rectangular square near the fort is the settlement of "Pittsboro." Number 9 is Detroit, another important British fort in the region. The turtle image is thought to be a reference to a Munsee creation story in which the world is supported on the back of a turtle.

Fort Pitt Daybook

Commerce, not warfare, was the most common contact between Native Americans and Europeans. The day book of the prosperous Baynton, Wharton and Morgan trading firm at Fort Pitt (1765-1767) illustrates how the seasonal orientation of native societies dictated trading: sporadic through winter till late spring, when hunting slowed for planting; heaviest during mid-summer's plenty; slowing again for harvest, its related ceremonies, and preparations for fall hunts.

Indians traded pelts (more than half from deer, with beaver, bear, otter, and raccoon also) for manufactured items such as lead bars, guns, clothing (including silk handkerchiefs, ruffled and calico shirts), gunpowder, needles, knives, food, ribbon, utensils, and paint.

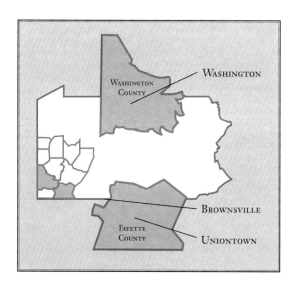

ther rugged, rocky, or stoney...." Predominately English settlers from Virginia and Maryland, and German, Irish, and Scots-Irish settlers from eastern Pennsylvania and New Jersey, came – not all voluntarily. Some Virginia and Maryland settlers supported Virginia's claims to the territory, and brought slaves who worked as farm laborers or domestic servants. Easterners supported Pennsylvania's claim to the territory in its dispute with Virginia; some also brought indentured servants.

These settlers quickly claimed and competed for the best lands along the creek and river valleys. Most people worked as farmers. German, Irish, and English farmers clustered together, providing a sense of community as they traded products and services. As the river valleys became more settled, latecomers moved towards the interior and border townships of Washington, Westmoreland, and Allegheny counties in search of land. As early as 1780, land ownership was not affordable to one-third of the population. This figure increased in the 1790s.

In the 1780s, most farmers lived by subsistence; few had advanced to commercial farming. A small group of landowners accumulated wealth in the form of large acreages, large herds of livestock, gristmills, and other businesses. The biggest owners, those with more than 400 acres, accumulated greater wealth during the 1780s, but only about 11 percent of the largest landowners added to their holdings in the next decade. People already familiar with the area – many former soldiers or military appointees, such as George Morgan – returned to Western Pennsylvania in the 1790s and accumulated large tracts of land. In a number of instances, the government had deeded them land as payment for military service.

Slave ownership was another sign of wealth. Although slavery was declining in Pennsylvania by the 1780s, it had some strength among wealthy settlers in Western Pennsylvania. Pennsylvania's Gradual Abolition Act required all slaves be registered, or else considered free, and placed other stipulations on the holding of slaves which ensured that the practice could not survive.

Commercial and subsistence farmers produced a surplus of grains, especially rye. Commercial farmers, hampered by the Appalachian Mountains, sold their surplus grains to the army or in rapidly growing settlements in Kentucky and Ohio. Nearly all farmers distilled their rye into whiskey, which became a main cash crop and, locally, a medium of exchange. One out of every six Western Pennsylvania farmers operated a still. "Monongahela Whiskey" was carried in 8 gallon kegs by pack horse, and sold in the East. Important items such as salt, lead, iron, and gunpowder were purchased for the return trip.

When the federal government enacted an excise tax on domestically produced whiskey in 1791, it had a devastating economic effect in Western Pennsylvania. Writing to William Young, Charles Nisbet wrote in 1792 that

> My friend Mr. Turnbull is concerned in a Distillery at Pittsburgh, but dare not make any Use of it, as if on the one hand he should pay the Duty, nobody would buy his Goods...and on the other hand, if he should distill, and not pay the Duty, his Goods would be liable to be seized by Order of Government & himself liable in heavy fines....

Petitioning the government, residents in Western Pennsylvania and in several other frontier areas protested with generally peaceful measures at first. For two years, federal officials in Philadelphia responded to these petitions, and made adjustments to the law, but officials misunderstood frontier grievances. Frontiersmen felt cut off from the governmental process. Excise resistance erupted across the western frontier. Hoping that these remote regions would fall into line, the federal government decided to quell excise resistance in Western Pennsylvania in 1794. George Washington mounted a 12,000-man army that marched west to quell the "insurrection." No rebel army took the field, and the confrontation ended with several isolated incidents of violence. Ironically, the Army needed provisions, and local farmers supplied these goods. Again, the military's impact on the region's economy was felt: many farmers bought additional land with the Army's cash.

By the 1790s, the region had 18 towns – nine in Fayette County, eight in Washington County and Pittsburgh. Such towns served as centers for exchanging goods and services – an essential role if the region was to sustain a more settled economic structure with which to attract larger numbers of people. In 1783, seven years after its founding, Uniontown in Fayette County had 20 artisans and shopkeepers. Towns drew together artisans, professionals, and demand for a wide variety of skills and services. A second important function of towns was to provide economic opportunities for the lower classes. Individuals who could not pursue agricultural occupations found work in towns. Some towns also served as educational and cultural centers, while others served as seats of local government. Both factors were to aid Pittsburgh's growth.

"Portrait of Dr. Peter Mowry"
Artist unknown, c. 1810
Peter Mowry began his apprenticeship in 1784 to the town's first physician, Nathaniel Bedford, and was a leading physician in the city until his death in 1833.

"We want people, we want sober and diligent tradesman: hatters, and button makers, weavers, etc. will be more welcome and will effectually promote our prosperity...."

— John Scull, editor of the
Pittsburgh Gazette, April 1789

"Portrait of John Campbell Plummer"
Artist unknown, c. 1850
John Plummer (1788-1873) started his adventurous merchants' career as a teenager. In 1805, he and his brother traded food and whiskey by boat along the Big Kanawha River in present day West Virginia. In 1810, Plummer took 300 barrels of flour, whiskey, and bacon to New Orleans via river. Continuing to Cuba, he traded for coffee, then bought a schooner and sailed to Philadelphia, returning by wagon to Pittsburgh. He also owned gristmills and sawmills. In 1830, Westmoreland County voters elected him as a state representative, and he also served three years (1839-1842) as a state senator.

Towns provided a more complex occupational structure. They attracted a small professional class of lawyers, doctors, teachers, and ministers, followed by a sizable mercantile class. Farmers accounted for 8 percent of the population, followed by a dependent class of day laborers, widows without land, the poor, and landless farmers. Artisans comprised the largest occupational class. In general, river townships had more artisans than interior or border townships.

The residents transformed Western Pennsylvania into a commercial and manufacturing center. Isolated by mountain roads that made the importation of fragile and heavy goods from the East difficult, entrepreneurs began to develop the means locally to produce items such as glass and furniture. A stable population and settlers passing through Western Pennsylvania on their way west also drove demand for locally made consumer goods. An abundance of natural resources, including lumber, coal, salt, and water as a source of energy and transportation were enviable attributes as Western Pennsylvania grew as a manufacturing center.

During the 1770s and 1780s, the military had attracted gunsmiths, blacksmiths, boat-builders, and other artisans to Pittsburgh to manufacture and repair military goods. Thomas Ashe, a British traveler, noted that militarily, Pittsburgh was "the key to the western country." The Ohio River provided an easy means to transport military goods and soldiers west. This would help to establish the city's reputation as a trading and artisan center, though an economy of merchants and manufacturers — one far less dependent on the military — did not develop until the turn of the 19th century.

Pittsburgh, with a population of only 376 in 1790, had one clock- and watch-maker, two tanners, four cabinetmakers, two hatters, two weavers, five blacksmiths, five shoemakers, three saddlers, and a few other skilled artisans by 1792, according to the *American Museum* periodical. The city retained its frontier flavor throughout the decade, and Uniontown and Washington and Brownsville in Washington County rivaled Pittsburgh in population, refinement, and industrial development. By the mid-1790s, Uniontown had potters, tailors, a breeches maker, a brewer, and a silversmith. In 1792, according to *Universal Magazine*, Pittsburgh had more artisans than Washington, but the latter had a greater variety. The magazine listed artisans with 23 different skills operating in Washington, while Pittsburgh had 17.

But Pittsburgh quickly dashed ahead of its rivals, due largely to its location at the junction of three rivers – the Allegheny, Monongahela, and Ohio. After 1800, people flowed through Pittsburgh in numbers greater than ever imagined, and glassworks, mills, and merchants competed for space and resources. Pittsburgh had 1,500 residents in 1800, and 60 shops. Food, clothing and everyday consumer goods were readily available. Coffee, chocolate, molasses, and other luxury items, though predictably expensive, were also available. Those who lacked hard cash could barter butter, eggs, grains, and other essentials.

Pittsburgh became more than an economic and transportation hub. In 1786, Henry Hugh Brackenridge had rhapsodized about "halls lighted up with splendor, ladies and gentlemen assembled, various music, and the mazes of the dance." In 1787, the Western University was founded. Within a few years, numerous girls' boarding schools had opened, Edgeworth's being the best known. Mathematics, history, botany, French, geography, and elocution were taught. Each session ran 22 weeks and cost $66. Drawing and painting were taught at an extra cost. The city became a stop for traveling theater troops and concerts, and quickly developed its own fine art diversions. In the early 1790s, the city had a music teacher, and by 1820, numerous instructors in the arts.

Neither strategic military location, nor glass factories, river trade, or skilled artisans would likely have been enough for Pittsburgh to reach its perch as the region's most important new city. It was all of these factors, *plus* an educational and cultural dimension, which set Pittsburgh apart.

Margaret Bunyan Morgan's recipe book
Margaret Bunyan Morgan brought the family's recipe book with her when she moved in 1796 to Washington County from New Jersey. Recipes calling for exotic ingredients testify to the family's wealth and sophistication. (Morgan's father-in-law was Col. George Morgan, see p. 11.) But phonetic spellings and simple techniques and ingredients suggest a thorough acquaintance with more common fare, such as roast rabbit:

> Lay the [rabbits] down in a modirate fier – bast them with butter and dredge them with flower – melt some butter – boil the liver with a bunc of parsley – chop them fine – put half into butter – pour it in dish – garnish it.

The book also contains home remedies, including a cough suppressant:

> Take a large handfull of camimile flowers, an equil quantity of white balsam – boil them in a quart of water untill it is wasted to a pint – strain it and put it in a pint of brown sugar – let it boil to a syrup.

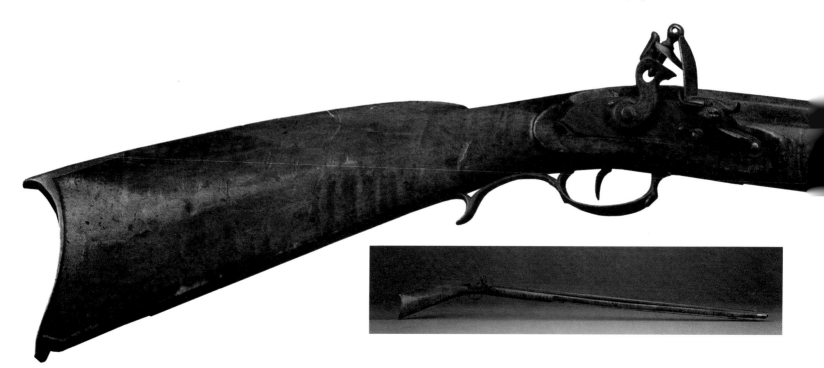

George Morgan silk waistcoat

Distinctive designs on George Morgan's silk waistcoat (c. 1790) evoke the eclectic pursuits of one of Western Pennsylvania's most unusual frontiersmen. A career begun as a trader ended as a fruit grower and farmer in Washington County.

As a western agent for the Baynton, Wharton and Morgan trading company in the 1760s, George Morgan acquired an understanding of Native American culture. During the American Revolution, as agent for Indian affairs at Fort Pitt, he worked to maintain peace on the western frontier. He advocated a withdrawal of whites from Kentucky, in exchange for peace in Western Pennsylvania. John Killbuck, a Delaware Indian, called Morgan "the wisest, faithfullest, and best Man I ever had anything to do with," but settlers did not like his proposals. He was discharged at Fort Pitt in 1779.

He returned to the area in 1796 with his son and daughter-in-law (see p. 10) and purchased the land for his estate, "Morganza."

1805 Map of Pittsburgh

William Masson's drawing of October 1805 reveals a town ready to expand in all directions. The Pittsburgh Market (center) was the square where area farmers sold eggs, meat, flour, and other produce. The fashionable residential district was between Liberty and Penn streets. Boat-building – both flat-bottomed river craft and ocean-going riggers – was an important early industry, and the map shows a shipyard on the Monongahela River. Masson drew ships heading down-river to emphasize Pittsburgh's prominence as a transportation hub.

Fowling rifle, c. 1782

A "fowling rifle" was an essential tool of the frontier family because turkey, quail and other fowl were staples. Owned by the David Shaw family of Westmoreland County (c. 1782), this flintlock weapon was made in Lancaster, Pa.

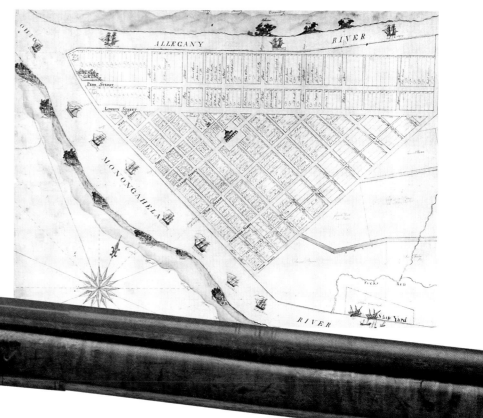

Tar and feathering an excise officer
artist unknown, c. 1794
Some Western Pennsylvanians reacted violently in 1791 when the federal government imposed a tax on the chief export of the region: whiskey. During the ensuing "Whiskey Rebellion," a local tax officer, John Neville, had his house burned to the ground. Another federal excise officer was tarred and feathered. Insurrectionists, whose peaceful petitions had failed, felt the tax violated hard-won liberties of the recent Revolutionary War. Federal officials sent troops to the region, finally quelling the rebellion.

Samuel Davis tall case clock

In a career spanning three decades, Samuel Davis became a famous Pittsburgh watch-maker perhaps known best for tall case clocks (this one, c. 1810). Between 1806 and 1826 alone, he reportedly made 97 clocks. Davis arrived from Ireland sometime before January 1795, according to his personal papers, but did not become a naturalized U.S. citizen until 1802. His sponsor was an uncle, John Johnston, a Pittsburgh clock-maker and silversmith whom Davis joined in business. In 1806, however, Johnston assumed the duties of postmaster; Davis placed an advertisement in the *Pittsburgh Gazette* of August 11:

> Samuel Davis
> Having dissolved partnership with Mr. Johnston,
> has commenced the
> Clock, Watch & Silversmith
> Business,
> *In Market Street between Second and Third
> Streets, opposite Mr. Spencer's Tavern.*
> Attention to this bussiness [sic], in it various
> branches, together with *Hair Work*, executed
> in the neatest manner, he flatters himself, he
> will receive a share of the public patronage.
> Pittsburgh, August 11th, 1806.
> N.B. The highest price given for old gold
> and silver.

Davis is listed in the 1815, 1819, and 1826 Pittsburgh city directories. On September 14, 1816, he advertised in the Pittsburgh Gazette that he had in his "employ a gentlemen lately from Paris, and has in his power to repair Watches and Timepieces of all descriptions in the best manner and on the shortest notice..."

Charles Rosenbaum pianoforte, c. 1815

Pianos of this style, made in Pittsburgh by Charles Rosenbaum (c. 1815), suggest a high standard of living and a settled, cultured gentility — household space dedicated to pursuit of the "finer arts" — not predictable in early city development.

Rosenbaum, who advertised his pianos in 1815 for $250 to $350 ($2,200 to $3,000 in 1995 dollars), is believed to have worked in Pittsburgh only a few years, but no information is available on where he came from. Notices in 1814 in the *The Mercury* (June 1, 8, 15) announced he had "lately established himself as a piano forte maker in this town," but within two years, the *Pittsburgh Gazette* (January 20) reported that his shop had burned. It is not known what became of him. Rosenbaum is listed in the 1819 city directory, but he does not appear in the U.S. census of 1790, 1810, or 1820.

Andrew Osthoff hollowware teapot, c. 1815 & Joseph Lukey sugar tongs, c. 1820

By 1815, skilled artisans in Pittsburgh manufactured silverware, and watches and clocks, among other things. Local demand for luxury goods is evidence of the city's early wealth, but little is known about the craft-work system except that apprenticeships with individual artisans often lasted many years.

Andrew Osthoff, a gold and silversmith, came from Baltimore around 1814. His shop, listed in the 1815 *Pittsburgh City Directory*, was on the east side of the downtown market. "A. Osthoff/Pittsburg" is stamped on the bottom of his hollowware teapot (c. 1815). By 1818, according to a May 27 advertisement that year in the *Pittsburgh Gazette*, there were new developments at Osthoff's firm:

> Modelena Osthoff, Widow of the late A. *Osthoff*, deceased, returns her grateful acknowledgments to the public for the favours shewn to her late husband, and begs leave to inform the citizens of Pittsburgh and its vicinity, that she intends carrying on the business in all its branches, at the old stand in Diamond alley, where she has on hand a great variety of Plate and Jewellery."

The widow and Joseph Lukey, who worked in the shop, then ran the business. Silver sugar tongs are stamped "Lukey." He died in the early 1820s, and while a probate inventory names his wife as Magdelena Lukey, it is unclear what became of the business.

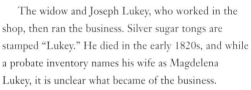

Annotated Bibliography

Primary Sources:

Regimental Book of the First Regiment, 1785-1789, in the Denny-O'Hara Papers, Mss. #51, Historical Society of Western Pennsylvania, provides details (names, ethnicity, occupation, and ages) of the 759 men who joined the first American regiment in 1785. Also included is information on discharges, trials, deaths, desertions, and the movement of companies among forts in the Ohio Country. James O'Hara's Military Contracting Business Papers, c. 1790s, also in the Denny-O'Hara Papers, HSWP, includes contracts, daybooks, and papers which document O'Hara's business relations with local and national individuals to supply and transport provisions to western forts.

The Fort Pitt Daybook, 1765-1767, HSWP, documents the intercultural trade between Native Americans and Europeans at Fort Pitt in the mid-1760s. It also documents the diversity of European material goods that Native Americans received, and it illustrates how seasons of the year dictated trade items; furthermore, the daybook documents the early material culture of Western Pennsylvania.

The Fort Pitt Daybook, 1779-1781, HSWP, documents the diversity of individuals who worked in the military. It lists the wages the military paid for services, including pay to surgeons, spies, agents, and militias.

The Pittsburgh Gazette, 1786, 1787, HSWP.

Pittsburgh City Directory, 1815, HSWP.

U.S. Manuscript Census, 1790.

Secondary Sources:

Bartlett, Virginia, *Keeping House: Women's Lives in Western Pennsylvania*, 1790-1850 (Pittsburgh: Historical Society of Western Pennsylvania and the University of Pittsburgh Press, 1994).

Harper, R. Eugene, *The Transformation of Western Pennsylvania*, 1770-1800 (Pittsburgh: University of Pittsburgh Press, 1990).

McConnell, Michael, *A Country Between: The Upper Ohio Valley and its Peoples*, 1724-1774 (Lincoln, Neb.: University of Nebraska Press, 1992).

Purvis, Thomas L, "Patterns of Ethnic Settlement in Late Eighteenth-Century Pennsylvania," *Western Pennsylvania Historical Magazine 70*, No. 2 (April 1987): 107-122.

Skelton, William B., "The Confederation's Regulars: A Social Profile of Enlisted Service in America's First Standing Army," *William and Mary Quarterly*, Oct. 1989, 770-785.

Slaughter, Thomas P., *The Whiskey Rebellion: Frontier Epilogue to the American Revolution* (New York: Oxford University Press, 1986).

Wallace, Anthony F.C., *Death and Rebirth of the Seneca* (New York: Vantage Press, 1969).

Green milk pan, and the Bakewells greyhound tumbler

Before iron and steel there was Western Pennsylvania glass. Utilitarian wares, such as milk bowls, and decorative pieces were produced. In 1828, British traveler Anne Royall visited the city's Bakewell, Page & Bakewell glassworks. She remarked about exquisite engraving work, "surpassing any I have seen in the country... particularly a *grey-hound*... perfect and entire, the ears, nose, and eyes were life itself."

Gradual Abolition Act

The Gradual Abolition Act of 1780 ordered owners to register slaves, and to free all slaves born after March 1, 1780 within 28 years. In Western Pennsylvania, enforcement was delayed until settlement in 1783 of a three-decade-long boundary dispute with Virginia. Allegiances to slavery were divided in Western Pennsylvania. Many settlers from Virginia* and Maryland held slaves; most Quakers from eastern Pennsylvania wanted the western region free of the "foul legacy."

Registrations in 1783 document 795 slaves in Westmoreland County and 443 in Washington County. The act's profound impact was apparent by the first U.S. census in 1790: 128 slaves in Westmoreland, 265 in Washington. Slave-holding had also declined in Fayette and Allegheny counties: by 1800, the census listed 79 slaves in Allegheny County; by 1840, there were no slaves in the county.

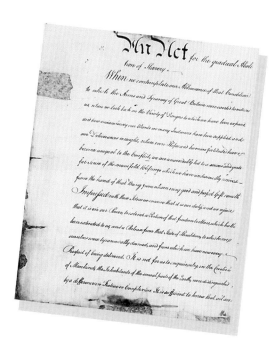

John Huey slant-front desk

In the 1790s, Western Pennsylvania developed into a manufacturing center. A wide variety of furniture – desks, chest of drawers, tables, and bookcases – were made. For this desk, John Huey used walnut and cherry, with inlaid walnut and poplar, all common woods in Western Pennsylvania. Signed local pieces are rare, but on a drawer bottom, in cursive ink, Huey's notations are found (inset).

Boyar had come from New Jersey in the early 1790s, and had purchased a farm in northern Washington County. Boyar and his wife, Nancy, had five children. In 1793, Boyar, although he was a Quaker, registered one slave.

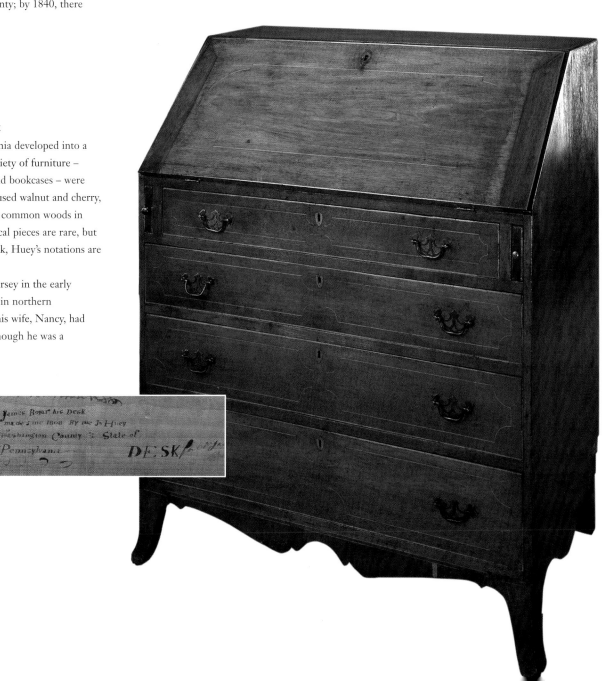

"View of the City of Pittsburgh in 1817"
by Emma Gibson
While on her 1817 honeymoon with her husband, Jason
Gibson, a Philadelphia lawyer, Emma Gibson sketched one
of the earliest known views of Pittsburgh. It dramatizes
how geography confined and restricted the city to the flat
land around the Point, and shows industrial development
along the rivers. In the right background, along the
Monongahela River, is the Bakewell Page & Bakewell
glassworks. (The building of the Monongahela Bridge in
1818 marked the start of city expansion beyond the flat
triangle). Boats in the foreground, heading up the Ohio
River, emphasize this link to western towns.

CHAPTER 2

City on the Move

1815-1875

Essay & Captions by Anne Madarasz

"The Point of Pittsburgh"
by William Coventry Wall, c. 1840
Pittsburgh's strategic location on three rivers figured heavily in its commercial development, and Wall documents that relationship. His rendering of detail at water level reinforces the importance of the rivers in the city's early history and captures the constraints of the surrounding hills.

By 1840, Pittsburgh supported a small community of artists. William Wall and his brother Alfred immigrated in the 1820s from Oxford, England. The family settled in Mt. Pleasant, Fayette County. William came to Pittsburgh in 1843 to work at J.J. Gillespie's Variety Store, America's first art gallery. Best known for two paintings of Pittsburgh after the fire of 1845, Wall left a pictorial legacy of city life at mid-century.

Flatboats
Flatboats and keelboats were the primary means of river transport before the age of steamboats. Keelboats were long and narrow, of light draft, for shallow waters. Flatboats, of sturdier build for travel on the Mississippi, were about 60 feet long and cost $75 to build. Doubling in cost and length by the 1850s, with up to a 150-ton capacity, flatboats owned by merchants or farmers were operated by deck hands and a professional pilot. Keelboats could be polled upstream, but flatboats were designed strictly for downstream use.

Imagine arriving in Pittsburgh in 1815. Coming from the east, the trip was seven days through the mountains on rough, muddy roads. Civilization must have been a welcome sight. If it is spring, this town of 10,000 residents is teeming with strangers waiting to ride the high waters west. Steamboats, having just been introduced on the Ohio River, are available for the journey. Many people, though, will still hop a ride on a keelboat or flatboat. All types of goods are stacked in the warehouses along the Monongahela Wharf – from food to hand tools produced in the region. If you have money, local artisans can provide the finer things as well – silver, watches, flint glass, or even a pianoforte from Charles Rosenbaum. Wisps of smoke rising from homes and mills remind you that this is coal country, where every man can afford to be warm.

Now imagine arriving 60 years later, in 1875. Your trip could be made by train and measured in hours, not days. You will also find a very different city. Bridges link downtown with the mills of Birmingham (South Side) and small businesses and breweries across the Allegheny in Allegheny City (North Side). Pittsburgh is

Sterling silver presentation tray

Irish creditors of Pittsburgh entrepreneur Michael Allen presented him this tray, made by Grays of Dublin (1839), in appreciation. After immigrating to Pittsburgh around 1815, Allen specialized in emerging fields of commerce. Working on commission, he bought, sold, and shipped local and regional products (Kentucky tobacco, bacon, lumber, flour) to growing western markets. Other interests included the city's first steam-powered textile mill (Phoenix Cotton Mill), steamboats, banking, and insurance. With wife Sarah, he even ran "Lucky Lottery" offices. In less than 20 years, he would pay off old debts in his homeland.

Early glass — flask and mineral water bottle, c. 1830-70

The region's first glass factory, Albert Gallatin's in New Geneva, opened in 1797. The O'Hara-Craig factory opened a few months later in Pittsburgh at the foot of Coal Hill, now Mt. Washington, using the cheap and abundant coal for fuel. Bottles and window glass, essential on the frontier but too fragile to be brought over the Alleghenies, were the primary products. Pocket flasks usually carried whiskey, the favored drink of the period.

Broadside announcing opening of Monongahela Bridge (right)

In Pittsburgh, bridges as much as buildings define the cityscape. The first bridge, announces this broadside, opened in November 1818 across the Monongahela, linking downtown with Birmingham (now the South Side). Privately built, it had a gate on the Pittsburgh side, where William Hart collected the 2-cent fare (human or livestock). In the first month alone, Hart's account book shows, tolls totaled $741.45.

MONONGAHELA
BRIDGE.

Notice is hereby given, that the gates of this Bridge, will be opened on Saturday the 28th inst. for foot passengers, horsemen, carriages, empty waggons of any size, and loaded light waggons.

The following are the

RATES OF TOLL.

	Dols	Cts
Every foot passenger,		2
Every carriage of whatever description, used for the purpose of trade, or agriculture, having 4 wheels and drawn by 6 horses;	62½	50
Every such carriage drawn by 5 horses	50	43¾
Every such carriage, 4 horses	37½	37½
Every such carriage, 3 horses	31	25
Every such carriage, 2 horses	25	18¾
Every such carriage, 1 horse	20	12½
Every carriage used for the purpose of accommodation or pleasure, having 4 wheels and drawn by 4 horses,	62½	50
Every such carriage drawn by 2 horses,	50	25
Every such carriage, 1 horse,	31	12½
Every carriage drawn by oxen or partly by oxen and partly by horses to be rated in proportion of two oxen for one horse, and in all cases a mule shall be rated the same as a horse.		

	Dols	Cts
Every carriage of whatever description used for the purpose of trade, or agriculture, having 2 wheels and drawn by 4 horses,	37½	37½
Every such carriage drawn by 3 horses	31	25
Every such carriage, 2 horses	25	18¾
Every such carriage, 1 horse	18	12½
Every chair, or other two wheeled carriage of pleasure, for every horse used therein,	18	12½
Every sleigh or sled drawn by 4 horses	25	25
Every sleigh or sled 3 horses	20	20
Every sleigh or sled 2 horses	18	18
Every sleigh or sled 1 horse	12½	12½
Every horse, mare or gelding with rider	6	8
Every horse, mare or gelding without a rider	6	6
Every head of horned or muley cattle	3	3
Every head of sheep or swine	2	2

N. B. Not more than ten head of cattle will be permitted to pass in one drove.

Horses are not to go out of a walk on the Bridge.

JOHN THAW, Treasurer.

Pittsburgh, Nov. 26, 1818.

Butler & Lambdin, Printers.

First Train in Pittsburgh 1852

On December 10, 1852, the first locomotive from Philadelphia pulled into the East Liberty section of Pittsburgh, joining the cities by rail and reducing to 15 hours a trip that took the Thaw family seven days in 1804. Pittsburgh's position in a vast water network had dictated much of its early history, and transportation figured mightily in the new era. The railroad accelerated the movement of products and people, Pittsburgh became the center of U.S. steel rail production, and major railroad-related businesses were born.

Steamboat *New Orleans*

artist unknown

The *New Orleans*, the first steamboat on western waters, was launched in 1811 in Pittsburgh. Built at Beelen's Iron Foundry and financed by Robert Fulton and Robert Livingston, she worked the New Orleans-Natchez route until burning in 1814. Faster and more reliable, steamboats gradually replaced other craft. According to an 1836 analysis, 252 of the 300 steamboats built for western rivers came from Pittsburgh. Steam revolutionized inland travel and boosted the Pittsburgh region's commerce.

Woodworking planes

Planes and other woodworking tools were vital to settlers and craftsmen. Early in the nineteenth century, numerous artisans made and sold planes in the region. By the 1850s, however, Pittsburgh hardware stores were selling factory-made planes from Ohio and Connecticut. Marks of maker and seller on a tool are useful for tracing trends in production and merchandising.

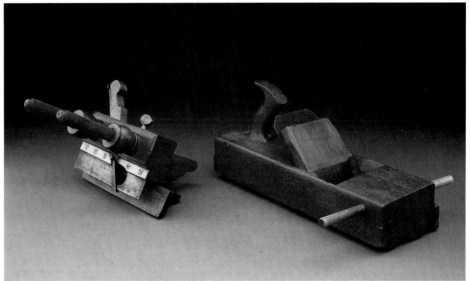

Fire company parade hats

Volunteer fire companies participated in street celebrations and parades. Companies originally were exclusive organizations – Eagle Fire Engine and Hose Company was the first (1794) – but gradually they opened their ranks. By 1845, the year of the great fire that devastated downtown, volunteers were known as much for drunkenness and brawling as for fighting infernos. On July 10, 1845, three months after the fire, both the Vigilant and Washington Fire companies marched through the streets of Pittsburgh and Allegheny in full regalia. Not until 1870 did Pittsburgh municipalize its firefighting.

"Great Conflagration at Pittsburgh, Pa. April 10 1845"

by James S. Baillie, lithographer, 1845

The great fire destroyed many of the city's buildings – 1,000 buildings and 700 homes, including many city landmarks. The Monongahela Bridge (burning in the center of illustration) from downtown to Birmingham on the river's south side had stood for 27 years; it burned "in eight minutes," said traveler Esther McComb. "There was a streak of fire clear across it as it still was burning in the water." Devastating urban fires were not uncommon in nineteenth century America. Their impact pushed cities to form municipally operated professional fire companies.

Wooden gas main, c. 1875

Before metal pipe there was wood. This piece, 7 inches in outside diameter and almost 18 inches long, came from under Fourth Street in Warren, in the region of northern Pennsylvania where America's oil and natural gas industry began. Pittsburgh, in 1873, was the first major U.S. city to be supplied with gas (from the "Haymaker" well near Murrysville in eastern Allegheny County). Before the decade was over, gas was industry's fuel of choice.

Template for Allegheny Arsenal Sign

This wood template for the iron sign hung on the gatehouse of the Allegheny Arsenal in the city's Lawrenceville district. Designed by Benjamin Latrobe and built in 1814, the arsenal supplied the military on the western frontier. In 1862 at this vital Civil War depot, an explosion killed dozens of young Lawrenceville women hand-rolling rifle cartridges. A heavy industrial base earned Pittsburgh renown as the "Arsenal of the Union."

Plaid Dress (left)

Irish immigrant Annie Butterfield wore this dress at her wedding in the 1850s. She and her husband operated a dairy farm in what is now Schenley Park in Oakland. Many of the Irish immigrants to Pittsburgh in the 1840s and 1850s worked in agriculture, though hundreds also turned to the growing iron and steel works. At one-fifth of the city's population, the Irish were the largest immigrant group by 1850. Estimates are that about 70 percent of the city's working class were immigrants – one-third Irish, one-fourth Germans, and 10 percent English, Welsh and Scottish.

1872 Map of Birmingham

On the South Side, a narrow strip of Monongahela River flood plain, bustling iron and glass factories mingled with residences. Most industrial firms were relatively small: the mean number of employees was 27.9. Work forces increased due to equipment innovations in the 1870s and '80s, concentrating production among fewer firms and forcing others to relocate. Natural gas and rail lines made the outlying counties of Westmoreland and Washington particularly attractive to glass companies. A reliance on heavy industry had begun across the region.

Suggested Reading

Allen, Michael, *Western Rivermen, 1763-1861: Ohio and Mississippi Boatmen and the Myth of the Alligator Horse* (Baton Rouge: Louisiana State University Press, 1990).

Baldwin, Leland D., *The Keelboat Age on Western Waters* (Pittsburgh: University of Pittsburgh Press, 1941).

The Center for African American History and Culture, *Freedom and Community: 19th Century Black Pennsylvania* (Philadelphia: Temple University Press, 1992).

Couvares, Frances, *The Remaking of Pittsburgh: Class and Culture in an Industrial City, 1879-1919* (Albany: SUNY Press, 1984).

Cramer, Zadok, *The Ohio and Mississippi Navigator* (Pittsburgh, 1802) and *The Navigator* (Pittsburgh, 1814; reprint, Ann Arbor, 1966).

Filippelli, Ronald and Sandra Stelts, "Sons of Vulcan: An Iron Workers Album," in Kathleen Collins, ed., *Shadow and Substance: Essays on the History of Photography in Honor of Heinz K. Henisch* (Bloomfield Hills, Mich.: Amorphous Institute Press, 1990).

Fitch, John A., *The Steelworkers* (Pittsburgh: University of Pittsburgh, 1989).

Havighurst, Walter, *River to the West: Three Centuries of the Ohio* (New York: G.P. Putnam's Sons, 1970).

Hays, Samuel P., ed., *City at the Point: Essays on the Social History of Pittsburgh* (Pittsburgh: University of Pittsburgh Press, 1989).

Ingham, John N., *Making Iron and Steel: Industrial Mills in Pittsburgh, 1820-1920* (Columbus: Ohio State University Press, 1991).

Innes, Lowell, *Pittsburgh Glass, 1797-1891: A History and Guide for Collectors* (Boston: Houghton Mifflin, 1976).

Lyford, W.G., *The Western Address Directory* (Baltimore: Jos. Robinson, 1837).

Pittsburgh City Directory, 1815 to 1875.

Reiser, Catherine Elizabeth, *Pittsburgh's Commercial Development, 1800-1850* (Harrisburg: Historical and Museum Commission, 1951).

Teaford, John C., *Cities of the Heartland: The Rise and Fall of the Industrial Mid-West* (Bloomington, Ind.: Indiana University Press, 1993).

Thaw Family Papers, Collection of the Historical Society of Western Pennsylvania.

U.S. Bureau of Census, manuscript census, 1820 to 1870.

Lyon, Shorb worker Joseph Weixel

Skilled craftsmen in the iron and glass industries represent a significant slice of Pittsburgh's economic pie in the mid-nineteenth century. Joseph Weixel, son of a Bavarian iron worker, labored with his brother Frank at the Lyon, Shorb Co. iron works. Cargo Studios of Pittsburgh was hired to photograph company workers in the mid-1860s. The photographs, mounted in an album, provide a rare glimpse of Pittsburgh's laboring classes.

Men such as Weixel spent 12 hours a day at the iron works. Probably recruited by his father, he learned his work as a boiler or puddler over several years, and because of this skill, exercised more control over work hours and pay than later industrial workers. A leader at work, he was also a leader in his South Side community, a founder of his neighborhood church, and an active member of its beneficent organizations.

Jos. Weixel

> *"Darkness gives the city a picturesqueness which [it] lacks wholly by daylight.... Around [its] edge and on the sides of the hills which encircle it like a gloomy amphitheatre,... through numberless apertures, fiery lights stream forth, looking angrily and fiercely up toward the heavens, while over all settles a heavy pall of smoke. It is as though one had reached the outer edge of the infernal regions, and saw before him the great furnace of Pandemonium with the lids lifted."*
>
> — William Glazier, "The Great Furnace of America," 1883

"Steel Mills at Night"
by Aaron H. Gorson
Among the millions fascinated by Pittsburgh's great mills was Aaron Gorson. The Lithuanian immigrant, trained as an artist in Philadelphia and in Paris, lived in Pittsburgh from 1903 to 1921. In numerous canvases, he explores the drama of industry.

CHAPTER 3

The Industrial City

1870-1930

Essay by Philip Scranton & Anizia Karmazyn-Olijar; Captions by Karmazyn-Olijar

By the late 19th century, even before its 100th birthday as a city, Pittsburgh had already been known nationally by a variety of catchy nicknames. But during the era of metals production that ensued on a scale more tremendous than ever seen on the face of the earth, writers would add another crisp characterization, one that spoke to the city's darker side: "Hell with the lid off." For generations after the 1880s, Pittsburgh's fire and smoke meant work and profits – hard, dangerous work for tens of thousands; handsome, tidy profits for an industrial elite.

Behind such durable images of the workplace, however, lay a more complex tapestry of regional industrialization, technological and market change, finance, immigration, community building, and reform. Bitter competition and conflict wove through that fabric, burning like a Bessemer blast, leaving holes and singed edges. Capitalists battled each other for markets; they all fought the railroads and unions, and courted or feared the bankers. Workers struggled after jobs and dignity, greeting each new, rival, in-migrating group with no little hostility, particularly the last – incoming black Americans.

**Mesta Machine Company,
West Homestead, c. 1910**
Mesta was a major employer in West Homestead, manufacturing some of the Industrial Age's largest pieces of steel-handling equipment.

Working-class women confronted grime, tissue-thin budgets, the perils of childbirth, and, too often, the sorrows of widowhood or abandonment. Hell with the lid off, indeed.

Yet despite these abiding tensions, and between recurrent flare-ups and depressions, these same people built industrial Pittsburgh. The elite funded technical transformations and product diversification that powered the steel trade to national leadership, while supporting its elegant downtown department stores, creating affluent neighborhoods, and sponsoring its peak cultural institutions. Workers fashioned the city's distinctive "districts" and the tight strings of towns that dotted the banks of Pittsburgh's three rivers. These people constructed scores of churches and ethnic community halls, along with the webs of association – informal and institutionalized – that sustained group identity and responded to individual tragedies. If life was often fierce, Pittsburghers took an equally fierce pride in their ability to stand the heat, eat the smoke, and stay the course.

"Heat" defined the heart of the regional industrial economy – in its steel mills, forges, and foundries, at its thousands of beehive coke ovens, or in its scattered window and pressed glass works, smelters, and pipe works. Elsewhere Americans might calmly mill wheat or spin yarn; but in the watershed of three rivers in Western Pennsylvania, Vulcan's work resounded amid the discomfiting counterpoint of winter frosts and mine damp. Here heat came from coal, mined chiefly along a great swath from the east to the south of the city, drawn in first along waterways, then by rail. These nearby coal sources, the rivers, and a growing railway network helped make industrialization a regional, not just a central city phenomenon. As Pittsburgh's riversides filled with factories, enterprisers increasingly located new facilities up the Allegheny and Monongahela and down the Ohio, creating or reshaping places like New Kensington, Donora, and Ambridge. Others built astride the rail system or extended it to establish "inland" plants at Swissvale, Trafford, or Wilkinsburg. Pittsburgh gradually became the regional financial and administrative center of an industrial dynamic that generated dozens of manufacturing towns. Crucial for steel in the region was a rail system connecting Westmoreland and Fayette counties' Connellsville coking coal district in the south, Lake Erie ore transfer points to the north, and national markets east and west to riverside furnaces and fabricating works.

The Connellsville district's rich seams of coal, ideal for hot-oven

Puzzle toys

Moravian immigrant mill worker Joseph Garba's toys of recycled wood (c. 1920), homemade for his children, evoke the "make-do" attitude needed to face a variety of deprivations – in the Old and New World. Simply made, pocket-sized toys were valuable in Garbas' working-class Ambridge, where time for childhood games was scarce. Mothers needed young daughters for household duties, while adolescent sons joined the ranks of laboring men.

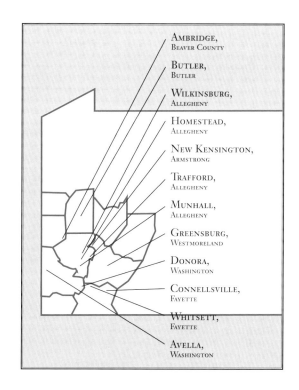

AMBRIDGE, BEAVER COUNTY

BUTLER, BUTLER

WILKINSBURG, ALLEGHENY

HOMESTEAD, ALLEGHENY

NEW KENSINGTON, ARMSTRONG

TRAFFORD, ALLEGHENY

MUNHALL, ALLEGHENY

GREENSBURG, WESTMORELAND

DONORA, WASHINGTON

CONNELLSVILLE, FAYETTE

WHITSETT, FAYETTE

AVELLA, WASHINGTON

Revolver

Pittsburgh was the scene again, in 1892, of violence between owners and laborers; management proposed to drastically reduce wages for skilled workers and union members at Carnegie Steel's Homestead Works. The "Battle of Homestead" was fought July 6. Among the workers was Herman Rohlecker, allegedly armed with the revolver shown here. He and hundreds of others fought 300 Pinkerton guards, hired by Carnegie's H.C. Frick, who arrived in river barges near the Homestead Works. More than 40 were killed or seriously injured.

"Capital and labor have clashed at Homestead, and the town is red with blood. Never in the bloody history of riots in this vicinity, save the great rail road riots of 1877, has there been such carnage and such a battle."

— *St. Louis Post-Dispatch*, July 6, 1892

transformation into steel-makers' coke, plus business links to Andrew Carnegie, made Henry Clay Frick a regional giant. (Later, bullets from anarchist Alexander Berkman almost "unmade" him.) Frick's coke fueled Carnegie's Edgar Thomson rail works, neatly located at a junction between the Pennsylvania and the Baltimore and Ohio railroads' main lines in Braddock, as well as his Homestead armor plate and specialty steel plant. The railroads both transported and used huge quantities of steel – chiefly thousands of tons of rolled rails for new and replacement track. At Homestead, unionized American, British, and German skilled workers had long governed the production processes. Carnegie's purchase of these works challenged their dominion, for he pledged to cut production costs, eliminate unions, and speed output of steels, so as to outpace his competition in price terms. In Spring 1892, with Carnegie safely abroad, Frick managed the harsh and bloody lockout that defeated the union, crushed workers' organizations for a generation, and opened the way both for decisive technical changes and for Berkman's attempt at revenge. Frick's 1892 comments about workers in his coalfields is classic: "Our experience has been such with organized labor that we could place no reliance on the agreements they made with us, and we concluded that we would end the thing once [and] for all, and determine whether we had the right to employ whom we pleased and discharge whom we pleased."

Management and labor in steel thus entered a century of conflict and mutual distrust that was matched by antagonisms between miners and coal operators. Yet "Carnegie" did not equal steel, and change involved more than smashing unions. Two main transformations governed the next 40 years – one in steelmaking processes, the other in markets. The Bessemer converter's fiery blast represented the difference between steel manufacturing and the old furnace-puddling of iron. The 1880s, however, saw the spread of the open-hearth furnace, a new steelmaking technique which much resembled iron puddling on a larger scale. Key to the adoption of open-hearth technologies was the higher quality of the steels produced (relative to Bessemer). Open-hearth steels were more durable and less likely to fail under strain, a characteristic critical to markets then developing. Among these, steels for structural forms in new skyscrapers and open-shed industrial buildings were of real significance, as were beliefs that open-hearth steels made better rails, armor, sheet, and plate, and offered better steel for castings (again displacing iron, this time in the foundry trades).

Moreover, an older, but smaller element in the Pittsburgh steel district received special attention at the century's turn. Crucible steel for metal-cutting tools well fit fabricators' needs for durable, high-speed devices that could rapidly shape varied components for machinery, machine tools, and automobiles. Rails had founded the steel industry; other demands would frame its further expansion in the Pittsburgh region.

This diversification of steel markets created avenues for success among the non-Carnegie cluster of firms, though some were absorbed into J.P. Morgan's buy-out of Carnegie, which created U.S. Steel and ridded the industry of Carnegie's predatory competitive tactics. Specialists in tool, structural, sheet, and customized forms found room to move outside the bulk rail and tonnage steel trades. In the same years, non-ferrous makers of lead, zinc, and most notably, aluminum, entered the regional mix. Their works were fueled by coal supplies, now increasingly turned to driving the steam turbines that provided electric power for factories, street lights, and homes. The coal-electric link was also facilitated by George Westinghouse's great Turtle Creek Valley plants, which supplied generators, turbines, switches, and railway-related components for the electrification of the region and the nation.

Between corporate leaders and factory workers, a new class emerged: bank staffers, managers, accountants, insurance assessors, and lawyers. These new middle-class professionals set themselves apart from the laboring masses and aspired to elite lifestyles. They, too, shopped at Kaufmann's, Horne's, and Gimbel's downtown, and enjoyed summertime long-distance vacations and regular trips to area amusement parks, baseball games, and concerts – all popular destinations on regional trolley lines. Yet they could not readily match the consumption options of their grander colleagues, for the elite occupied exclusive neighborhoods, special locales like Sewickley, Homewood, and Shadyside. Nor could they easily enter the social and business networks, the sets of boards of directors, that reinforced the power and action options possessed by Pittsburgh's leading families.

Many middle-class folks helped manage Pittsburgh's industrial companies, but a select few worked for its financial grandees such as the Mellons and their banker rivals. Massive needs for money beyond retained profits (so that technical advances could be funded) brought bankers a core role in Pittsburgh's development. Indeed, a half-dozen of them were counted among the city's early millionaires. Judge Thomas Mellon's T. Mellon and Sons Bank, founded in 1869, soon

Coal barges on the Monongahela
The three rivers, which earlier had moved freight and people west, clogged on the trade of the Industrial Age (here in downtown Pittsburgh, c. 1890). Barges shuttled coal and coke among mills and rail depots; rivers and rails linked outlying mines to urban industry.

provided Frick his first $10,000 loan, helping him onto the ladder to affluence. In the late 1880s, it was the Mellons to whom Alfred Hunt and Charles Hall appealed for funds to finance their aluminum reduction process, a step that founded what became Alcoa. However, Pittsburgh bankers were not always so accommodating and farsighted. For example, when George Westinghouse sought financing in 1891 to expand his already-vast electrical works, area bankers' demands were so stringent that he "went outside" to Wall Street's August Belmont, who assembled the necessary financial syndicate.

By the early years of the 20th century, banks were prominent among downtown's new office blocks and skyscrapers, which also housed the headquarters of Gulf Oil, the steel giants, and other leading firms. In 1917, Frick added the sumptuous Union Arcade Building, opening spaces for expanding legal and insurance enterprises and for exclusive specialty shops. Nearby clustered the city's fine hotels and grand department stores; not far distant was the Duquesne Club, where elite gentlemen dined, socialized, and judiciously discussed investments and trade.

Investing tens of millions created jobs by the tens of thousands, mostly hot and dangerous crew labor in factories and mines. To fill them, area companies recruited nationally and internationally; as a result, Pittsburgh's population tripled to 670,000 in the half-century after 1880. The influx of European immigrants and southern migrants produced a highly diverse, but overwhelmingly male, labor force for heavy industry. Earlier, families had come to the Pittsburgh area; these new arrivals tended to come alone. One Polish worker wrote home:

Now Dear Wife, I beg you to answer me, at least this letter, with a few words and inform me about your well-being and about my dear orphans, and if the youngest is already talking and walking well. I am terribly lonesome without my children and also without you. (Walter Borkowski, Pittsburgh, January 21, 1891)

Solitary workers also sent money orders to relatives at times. Their wait for a reply and perhaps a photograph could easily last four or five months.

Many immigrants and southern migrants hoped to return home and buy land with savings from their mill or mine earnings; but most gradually settled in Western Pennsylvania, bringing kin "across" or "up," or establishing new families. Newcomers sought greater economic opportunity and security; but, as their rural backgrounds poorly fitted them for traditional skilled positions, most found employment as low-paid laborers at often-dangerous work sites. Language problems added to the job hazards Central and Southern Europeans encountered. Outside the plants, there were further shocks. Thousands from farms or villages were quickly introduced to congested mill towns that afforded little room for comfort or leisure. Their lives were no longer governed by the rhythms of the seasons, but were dictated instead by the shift whistle's blasts and the twists of the business cycle.

With men spending 10- or 12-hour shifts in mills and mines, women became household managers, working equally demanding and exhausting hours. Many households included boarders from the "surplus" male population, men whose presence increased both family revenues and women's labors in cleaning, laundry, and food preparation. Families routinely had three to five children who lived to adulthood; work in and out of the home dominated their childhoods. Mothers taught daughters the tasks essential to maintaining a large household, while adolescent sons joined their fathers as wage-earners. The rudimentary schooling then available was unlovely. At Homestead in 1908, one first-grade teacher daily confronted the challenge of working with 68 students, sitting two to a desk, in her classroom.

Despite harsh living and laboring conditions, immigrants maintained their cultural traditions and rituals by erecting and attending "national" churches and by supporting a host of ethnic institutions (clubs, insurance societies, church lodges). Some ethnic small businesses provided traditional foodstuffs, beverages, and reading matter in

Danger sign in five languages
A one-year Allegheny County study begun in July 1906 recorded 526 workplace deaths, and an additional 509 injuries. Warnings in English, Italian, Hungarian, Slovak and Serbo-Croatian at Carnegie Steel's Homestead locomotive repair shop (c. 1910) seem gruesomely ironic: a typical work week was six or seven 12-hour shifts in fiery conditions with heavy equipment. Severed limbs, cripplings, and blindings were everyday threats.

multiple languages, while others offered private banking and savings options. Such institutions and activities affirmed immigrants' cultural identities in a new land, and more importantly, created opportunities for a range of social interactions outside the stresses of home and work.

Scattered mining towns offered the least appealing living conditions; but at some outlying sites, industrial corporations erected company-built housing when expanding or relocating their operations. When George Westinghouse launched his massive Trafford foundry, he sought to lure an able and skilled workforce by constructing several hundred solid homes on nearby tracts, rented at lower rates than available in the city. A few years later, another firm echoed this strategy, and announced:

> With the idea of preparing for the starting of a new car works in October, the Standard Steel Car Company has begun to build a large number of houses for its employees in close proximity to its new plant at Butler, Pa. A subsidiary... called the Lyndora Land Company... has plotted 150 acres of the 300 acres of [car company] land... and laid out 50 foot streets. Contracts were awarded for the building of 200 modern dwelling houses, which will be owned by the company and rented by workers. (*Butler Eagle*, July 2, 1902)

Of course, like miners, industrial workers living in company homes could be "put out" for insubordination or union activity, or displaced by layoffs in hard times; but better housing, some managers believed, drew better workers who might stay with the company for the long term.

This sentiment was far from general, however, as the Russell Sage Foundation's Progressive Era reformers discovered a few years later, when they brought the *Pittsburgh Survey* to Homestead and Munhall in 1907-08. Carnegie's land company built many homes at first, and continued to rent and maintain those in Munhall ("the best houses for the money in the town"). However, most later construction was left to private developers. The result was a split housing situation: one-quarter of Homestead's steelworker families owned their homes while the rest rented from landlords who enjoyed a tight market crowded with low-earnings families who could not afford higher rents for "improved" properties. Margaret Byington commented on the resulting situation:

> [Y]ou enter an alley, bordered on the one side by stables and on the other by a row of shabby two-story frame houses.

Photograph by Lewis W. Hine, "Wash Day in the Court"

Low factory wages for men forced families to take in boarders. Wives ran that business, juggling household finances and chores with tending children. New Yorker Lewis W. Hine was commissioned to photograph social conditions for the *Pittsburgh Survey*. His shot of wash day in a Homestead immigrant courtyard (c. 1910) captures the harsh realities of women's lives. Disguised as a laborer, Hine also photographed in the mills and mines.

The doors... are closed, but dishpans and old clothes decorating their exterior mark them as inhabited. [Next] you find yourself in a small court, on three sides of which are smoke-grimed houses.... The open space teems with life and movement. Children, dogs and hens make it lively underfoot; overhead, long lines of flapping clothes must be dodged. A group of women stand gossiping... awaiting their turn at the pump – which is one of the two sources of water supply for the 20 families who live here.... In the center a circular wooden building with ten compartments opening into one vault... constitutes the toilet accommodations for over one hundred people. (*Homestead: The Households of a Mill Town*, 1910)

Notwithstanding her genteel horror at such conditions, which were common but hardly universal in the region, Byington affirmed the deep desire of workers' families to own their own homes. Much was different when this was achieved. "When the house is paid for, the family often takes a genuine interest in its improvement," she wrote. "Sometimes it is the addition of a bathroom; sometimes repapering in the spring, which the busy mother finds time to do; sometimes the building of a washhouse in the yard. To plan and carry out these improvements always means the development of a sense of family life and its common interests."

One of the survey's supporters, Henry J. Heinz, invited researchers into his North Side food processing plant, the home of the famed "57 Varieties." Perhaps the city's largest employer of women, Heinz provided a clean and safe environment that, not incidentally, assured the purity of his canned and bottled products. Whereas Carnegie offered libraries to towns, Heinz's reformist impulses operated at the individual level. He promoted women line workers to clerical positions, installed a range of social services for his employees and for their children, and founded two settlement houses to develop youth programs. Of the last, Heinz noted in 1915: "We want to make this a factory for character building and good citizenship. It is our desire to surround the boys and girls of this neighborhood with such good influences that they will never want to depart from the right paths. Character, which is the outgrowth of honor, will be the goal of our endeavors."

Pittsburgh's middle-class women joined Heinz and others in pressing for reform, responding to the Survey's documentation of broadly

deplorable social, work, and living conditions. Though only mass unionization a generation later would address workplace issues (as the disastrous 1919 steel industry organizing strike showed), reformers moved forward on other fronts. They pressed for creation of playgrounds in working-class districts and for outdoor summer camps for working women, the latter generating thousands of young women's visits to a rural world of fresh air and open spaces that their parents had left long before. Retail firms employing women (Horne's, Kaufmann's) sponsored their own camps in the North Hills and at Bear Run, Pa. Others could "retreat" at the independent Pleasant Hill Farm Association camp, supported by female middle-class reformers. Inside the city, another local movement underwritten by wealthy businessmen fashioned the 300-plus acres of Schenley Park into an exemplar of modern, "City Beautiful" public spaces. Moreover, the business elite contributed additional funds to purchase and level parts of the adjacent, grubby Oakland district, thus clearing the way for establishing Pittsburgh's cultural and educational hub. By 1930, the Carnegie Museum, Library, and Institute, the University of Pittsburgh, Syria Mosque, and other facilities surrounded Forbes Field, that bizarre and much-missed arena for the Pittsburgh Pirates' triumphs and pratfalls.

Of course, the Pirates were were all white, and mostly native-born-like the city's business leaders, the reformers, and the social investigators, and unlike the region's industrial workers. Immigrant and black Pittsburghers, who labored and lived in the nearby Hill District,, occupied a different world.

Four postcards

1900-1920, with captions printed on them, of popular recreation spots in the Pittsburgh area (from opposite, top): Kennywood Park, Schenley Park Oval race track, West View Park, and Forbes Field.

Mill worker funeral

Mikolai Koval is laid to rest with his Greek Catholic Union hat and ribbon at St. Mary's Rusyn Greek Catholic Church, Johnstown, Cambria County. Koval was killed May 9, 1916 in a mill accident. Ribbons on lapels denote fellow members of Koval's fraternal lodge, which often used dues to pay death benefits to families. As well as membership benefits, ethnic fraternals offered immigrants social and cultural support.

Lace engagement cap, funeral scarf (above), and wedding photograph

Objects from home, especially those associated with life's momentous events, helped immigrants continue customs and rituals in Western Pennsylvania. Within two years of arriving in 1902 from the Slovakia region of Austria-Hungary, Mary Mejer, who brought with her a lace engagement cap and funeral scarf, had married George Rajcan in Braddock, near Pittsburgh. The family, in 1929, faced a tragedy that united newcomers of all nationalities when George Rajcan was fatally injured working at a steel mill.

Photograph, William Henry Mills

William H. Mills, dinner bucket in hand, headed for a day's work in Whitsett's mine (c. 1900). Mills, from Roanoke, Va., was part of the "Great Migration" of southern blacks to northern industrial jobs in the early twentieth century. Pittsburgh was among the top destinations; its African American population increased six-fold between 1870 and 1910 (4,459 to 34,217).

Braddock National Bank money order

Thomas Haraburda, a 1912 immigrant from Slovakia, sent money orders from earnings at the Edgar Thomson Works in Braddock to family back home (wife Alzbeta with their daughters and, at far left, Grandmother Anna Dova). Most single men returned home with their U.S. earnings to buy property, but often (an estimated 3 out of 10 cases) the earnings went to pay family members' passage to America. Successes encouraged others, resulting in "chain migration": the tendency for immigrants from a town in Europe to congregate in the same town or city neighborhood in Western Pennsylvania.

House #45 in Whitsett, Canning jar

Many immigrants preferred industrial work in the country to that in the city. The Toth family, Hungarian immigrants to Whitsett, "House #45" (1908), used grapes from their arbor for wine and preserves. Canning garden vegetables helped Hungarian immigrant Julia Orosz and neighbors through the winter. "Chow-chow" relish was Orosz's specialty.

"Our homes were two family houses, and each side contained two rooms upstairs and two rooms downstairs. We had no bathroom, no cellars, and no running water but we had a crawl space under our house where canned goods were kept. There was a coal shanty and an outside toilet which we shared with our neighbor, we used a Sears catalogue for toilet paper."

— Anne Moskal Pato grew up in Whitsett, Pa.

"Our school day started with Bible reading, the saying of the Lord's Prayer, the flag salute, singing and exercises."

— **Anne Moskal Pato**

Bird's-eye view of Whitsett

Towns such as Whitsett, Fayette County (c. 1915), sprang up around mines across the region. Much like factory-town counterparts, these miners' "patches" offered generally crude housing erected and rented by the mine company. Patches were often in remote locations, and the company's store stocked work supplies, household goods and food at inflated prices. Whitsett had a school, infirmary, and Baptist church.

Miner

Coal mine, Connellsville area, Fayette County, c. 1890.

Breaker boys among mining men

At Whitsett (c. 1910), Pittsburgh Coal Co. hired "breaker boys," 8 or 9 years old, to break unwanted slate by hand out of mined coal. Fathers took their sons into the mine to teach them the trade. Child labor was especially common before a federal law passed in 1916 began to restrict it.

"Twelve was the legal age for working in a mine in 1895, so it was decided that I would enter the mine with my father, to help increase the family income ....

As I walked into the mine with my father on my first day, I was reminded of a boy named Lindsay, a year or two older than I, who had been killed in the mine a few months before."

— John Brophy, an English immigrant boy, was a coal miner at Urey Mine in Indiana County, Pa.

"[I]t would take anywhere from an hour to a little better than an hour to walk out [of the mine]. But if you came out the main hall, they had an air shaft if you felt like walking one hundred and fifty feet up steps."

— Ben Erving, an African American miner, migrated from Alabama in 1923 and worked in Western Pennsylvania coal mines for 20 years.

Darr Mine explosion, 1907

An open flame lamp on a miner's cap was said to have caused the December 19, 1907 explosion that killed 200 deep inside Pittsburgh Coal's Darr Mine, Van Meter, Westmoreland County. It remains one of the nation's worst mining disasters. Flammable gases trapped in coal beds were among the many dangers of underground mining.

"The terrible force of the explosion was evidenced on the five bodies that were found along the road and brought to the surface. Every one was mutilated, in some cases arms or legs being missing. A considerable area about the mine was roped off to prevent the grief-frenzied relatives of the entombed men from crowding into the mine."

— *The Morning Review*, Greensburg, Pa., December 20, 1907

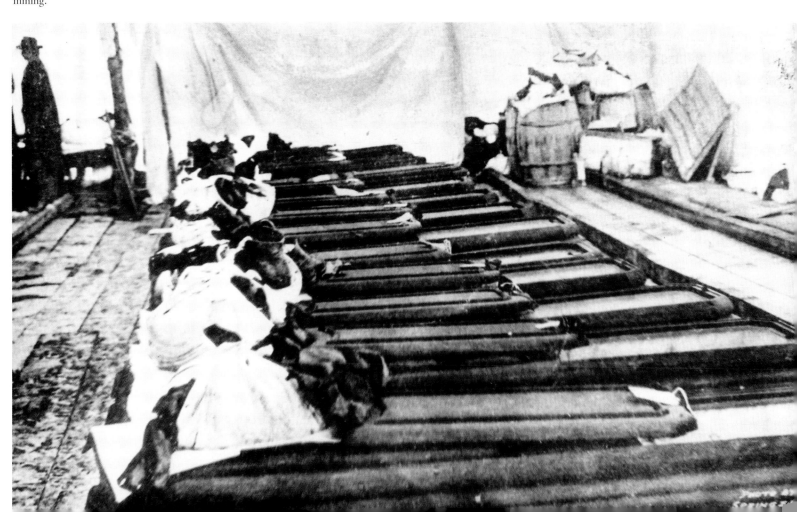

Cartoon in July 9, 1892 *Saturday Globe*, Utica, N.Y.

Andrew Carnegie's critics charged that he piled up money for philanthropy by paying low salaries to his workers, whose inhumane hours precluded them from enjoying his generosity. In his 1869 *Wealth*, the steel magnate had written that the rich are the keepers of culture; he beseeched all to accumulate wealth but to support good causes. Libraries bearing Carnegie's name were his top charity – 2,811 in America and Great Britain.

Miners organizing in Avella, Pa., 1925 (below)

Most attempts at unionization in the coal fields of the late 19th and early 20th centuries failed or were suppressed. But the movement gained momentum in the 1920s under the leadership of John L. Lewis. In Avella, Washington County, demonstrations in 1925 marked formation of a United Mine Workers of America local.

Alexander Berkman dagger

Seventeen days after the bloodshed at Homestead came revenge against the man whom many blamed. Alexander Berkman, a Russian immigrant with anarchist views sympathetic to oppressed workers, surprised industrialist H. C. Frick in his downtown office. Berkman shot Frick twice and stabbed him three times. He is said to have used this knife.

"Burning of Union Depot During the Railroad Riot July 21st and 22nd, 1877"

by William G. Armor, engraver, and Otto Krebs, lithographer

In 1877, railroads announced arbitrary cuts in pay and increased work loads that raised safety concerns among workers. A strike was promised, which, when it came, management, government, and newspapers called a "riot." Nationwide, more than 100 were killed. In Pittsburgh, railroaders and supporters clashed with Pennsylvania state militia at the depot on 28th Street. Vivid night-time fires caused widespread property damage in America's most bitter labor strife to date. The events established Pittsburgh, already famous as a city of mighty entrepreneurs, as a labor stronghold as well.

BURNING OF UNION DEPOT DURING THE RAILROAD RIOT JULY 21ST & 22ND 1877. PITTSBURGH. PA.
LIST OF KILLED.

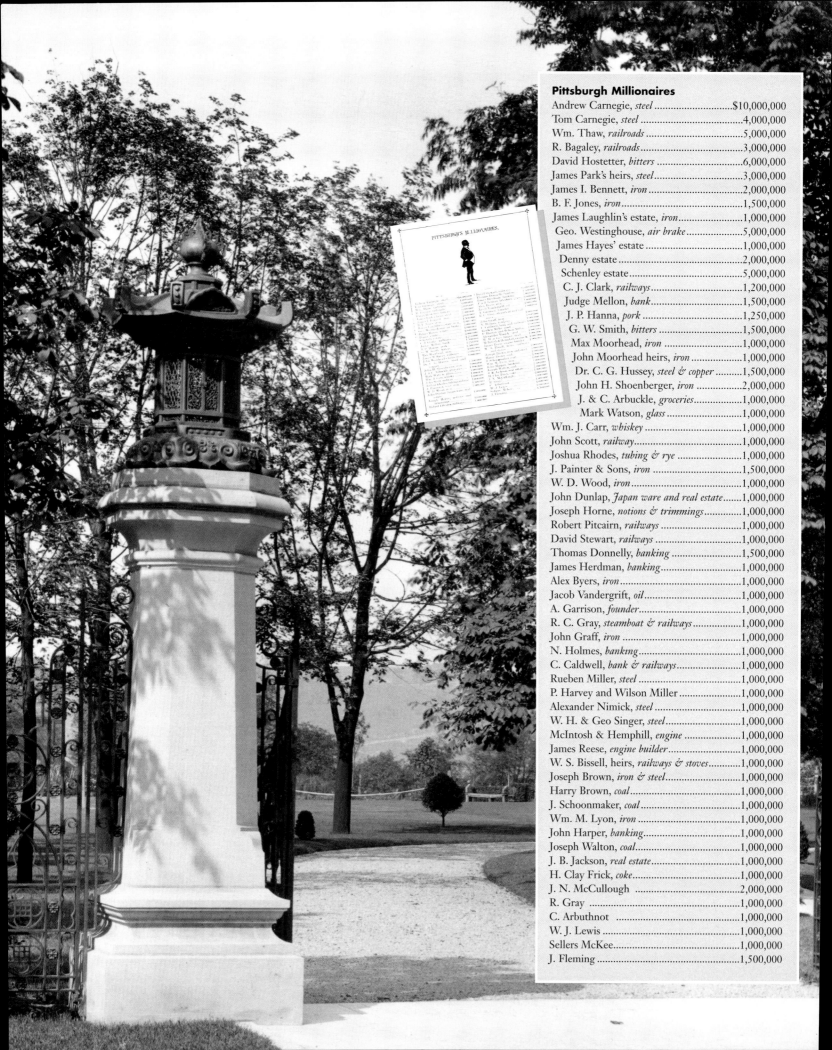

Pittsburgh Millionaires

Andrew Carnegie, *steel*	$10,000,000
Tom Carnegie, *steel*	4,000,000
Wm. Thaw, *railroads*	5,000,000
R. Bagaley, *railroads*	3,000,000
David Hostetter, *bitters*	6,000,000
James Park's heirs, *steel*	3,000,000
James I. Bennett, *iron*	2,000,000
B. F. Jones, *iron*	1,500,000
James Laughlin's estate, *iron*	1,000,000
Geo. Westinghouse, *air brake*	5,000,000
James Hayes' estate	1,000,000
Denny estate	2,000,000
Schenley estate	5,000,000
C. J. Clark, *railways*	1,200,000
Judge Mellon, *bank*	1,500,000
J. P. Hanna, *pork*	1,250,000
G. W. Smith, *bitters*	1,500,000
Max Moorhead, *iron*	1,000,000
John Moorhead heirs, *iron*	1,000,000
Dr. C. G. Hussey, *steel & copper*	1,500,000
John H. Shoenberger, *iron*	2,000,000
J. & C. Arbuckle, *groceries*	1,000,000
Mark Watson, *glass*	1,000,000
Wm. J. Carr, *whiskey*	1,000,000
John Scott, *railway*	1,000,000
Joshua Rhodes, *tubing & rye*	1,000,000
J. Painter & Sons, *iron*	1,500,000
W. D. Wood, *iron*	1,000,000
John Dunlap, *Japan ware and real estate*	1,000,000
Joseph Horne, *notions & trimmings*	1,000,000
Robert Pitcairn, *railways*	1,000,000
David Stewart, *railways*	1,000,000
Thomas Donnelly, *banking*	1,500,000
James Herdman, *banking*	1,000,000
Alex Byers, *iron*	1,000,000
Jacob Vandergrift, *oil*	1,000,000
A. Garrison, *founder*	1,000,000
R. C. Gray, *steamboat & railways*	1,000,000
John Graff, *iron*	1,000,000
N. Holmes, *banking*	1,000,000
C. Caldwell, *bank & railways*	1,000,000
Rueben Miller, *steel*	1,000,000
P. Harvey and Wilson Miller	1,000,000
Alexander Nimick, *steel*	1,000,000
W. H. & Geo Singer, *steel*	1,000,000
McIntosh & Hemphill, *engine*	1,000,000
James Reese, *engine builder*	1,000,000
W. S. Bissell, heirs, *railways & stoves*	1,000,000
Joseph Brown, *iron & steel*	1,000,000
Harry Brown, *coal*	1,000,000
J. Schoonmaker, *coal*	1,000,000
Wm. M. Lyon, *iron*	1,000,000
John Harper, *banking*	1,000,000
Joseph Walton, *coal*	1,000,000
J. B. Jackson, *real estate*	1,000,000
H. Clay Frick, *coke*	1,000,000
J. N. McCullough	2,000,000
R. Gray	1,000,000
C. Arbuthnot	1,000,000
W. J. Lewis	1,000,000
Sellers McKee	1,000,000
J. Fleming	1,500,000

"Greenlawn"

H.J. Heinz's "Greenlawn" shouldered in among the millionaires' estates on Penn Avenue in Point Breeze. Shadyside was another prestigious East End address, as was Sewickley, in western Allegheny County. In 1901, the year of U.S. Steel's formation, Pittsburgh banks held more receipts than several European countries, and the city was believed to be the world's richest ever.

Duquesne Club luncheon program

The downtown Duquesne Club, founded in 1873, was the spot for business socializing. Luncheons for dignitaries, such as the Crown Prince of Siam (November 5, 1902), called for monogrammed tableware (inset), Duquesne Club brand cigars, and exquisite programs. Such pomp confirmed for the business elite that they were important on a State level.

J&L Steel

Pittsburgh's Jones & Laughlin Steel Co. accounting department, 1909.

Wool and velvet opera cloak, c. 1900

Evening cultural events, such as a performance by the Pittsburgh Symphony or an opera company, called for appropriate and fashionable attire for ladies. A wool and velvet cloak (c. 1900) was a favorite.

Silk bodice and skirt (far right)

A black dress made of faille believed to have been worn by Nancy Davis (c. 1897) to her clerk's job at the Boggs and Buhl Department Store in Allegheny, Pa. She lived in the Troy Hill section of Pittsburgh.

Early cable car

Residential areas distant from downtown were served by horse-drawn buses and finally by electric streetcars and trolleys. By the late 1880s, "streetcar suburbs" offered new if not palatial housing for the managerial executives, professionals, and business owners of an expanding consumer economy. The 2.5-mile-long Pittsburgh, Knoxville, and St. Clair Street Railway, the city's first, operated mainly in new suburbs on the city's southern fringe. One study indicates that not until well into the 20th century was daily transit affordable for Pittsburgh's working class.

Phipps Conservatory

Entrepreneur and Andrew Carnegie associate Henry Phipps built a conservatory for Allegheny's citizens in 1887. Six years later, he built another, on the 300 acres that Mary Schenley had donated for a city park. Phipps Conservatory, a leading Schenley Park attraction, helped lead the dramatic 20th century transformation of Oakland into Pittsburgh's cultural district.

"[T]here is being constructed a building which will bear the distinction of being the largest and finest structure of its kind in the world. The paramount consideration from its conception being the comfort, convenience and satisfaction of its tenants, economy was not allowed to encroach upon either exterior beauty or interior excellence and utility. Everything conceivable by the mind of the master-builder wrought out by the hand of the skilled fellow craftsman, has been lavishly incorporated in the construction of the Union Arcade Building."

— Promotional brochure, 1916

Advertising brochure for Frick's Union Arcade Building, 1916 (left and above)

H.C. Frick hired Pittsburgh architect Frederick J. Osterling to design an ornate, world-class office tower at Sixth Avenue and Cherry Way downtown. Exclusive shops on the first four floors of the Union Arcade Building, finished in 1916, were geared to Pittsburgh's wealthy families. Numerous accounting, law and managerial firms also took up residence.

Joseph Horne Co.
PENN & FIFTH AVE'S.
Pittsburgh, Pa.

WRITING ROOM

Dear

Oct, 22 ~ 23 - 1933

JOSEPH HORNE CO.
PITTSBURGH
PENNSYLVANIA

Writing Room

Dear Rachel,

I had a few Errands and came in this morning to do them. I want to make a Pillow for Ann Hamilton for her coming out Lunch Nov, 1st. Nancy called up the other day & invited us with a few more older people to the Lunch. I think she is going to have about 60 people at Fox Chapel in the Dining room up stairs and about twelve of her own friends down stairs - I am sorry

Downtown appeal

The central city in the early 20th century was a bustling place. Among the dozen or so department stores, the clock on Smithfield Street outside Kaufmann's was a familiar landmark. Horne's, meanwhile, offered stationery and a room where leisure-class ladies like the sisters Rachel and Sarah McClelland (c. 1920) could break from their buying to pen letters to friends or relatives. They were daughters of Dr. James McClelland, Jr., "physician to the stars" in Pittsburgh, and founder of what is now Shadyside Hospital, not far from the family's Fifth Avenue mansion. Rachel McClelland became a well-known painter.

A country outing by car, c. 1905

Automobiles created options for leisurely, private, and spontaneous outings – though near Pittsburgh, the exact location pictured is unknown – that no streetcar could equal. Use of the car for commuting was predictable; by the time major public investment in area roads was completed in the 1920s, Americans' love affair with the auto was in high gear.

Suggested Reading

Brody, David, *Steelworkers in America: The Non-Union Era* (Cambridge, Mass., 1960); *Labor in Crisis: The Steel Strike of 1919* (Urbana, Ill., 1987 [reprint of 1965 edition]).

Byington, Margaret, *Homestead: The Households of a Mill Town* (Pittsburgh, 1974 [reprint of 1910 edition]).

Ingham, John, *Making Iron and Steel* (Columbus, 1991).

Misa, Thomas, *A Nation of Steel: The Making of Modern America* (Baltimore, 1995).

Serrin, William, *Homestead* (New York, 1992).

Wall, Joseph, *Andrew Carnegie* (Pittsburgh, 1989 [reprint of 1970 edition]).

Wolf, Leon, *Lockout* (New York, 1965).

Immigrants & Reformers

During the late 19th and early 20th centuries, the Hill District, a mile from the Golden Triangle's wealth, was Pittsburgh's most important new-immigrant district. A large portion of the city and its suburbs' families today trace their histories as Americans to the Hill. Shown in 1926 is Sidney Teller, executive director of the Irene Kaufman Settlement, considered historically to have been the Hill's most important charitable agency. He surveys conditions with a youngster off Crawford Street.

CHAPTER 4

The Hill: A City Neighborhood

1900-1940

Essay & Captions by Teresa Lynne Riesmeyer

Just east of Pittsburgh's downtown business district, running south to the bluffs of the Monongahela River and east to Oakland, lies one of the city's oldest neighborhoods. To those only familiar with the city since the 1950s, the Hill District is identified as an African American neighborhood with struggling commercial districts and dilapidated housing. Yet, the Hill's real legacy is not tied to one ethnic group, but rather to the sheer diversity of people – people from all parts of the world – who have called Ward 3 and Ward 5 home over the years. This chapter breaks from the more chronological narratives on either side of it to address a neighborhood that figures enormously in the peopling of modern Pittsburgh.

The early years of the century usually are remembered fondly by the blacks, Jews and Christians from a dozen European nations, Mediterranean and Middle Eastern natives, and Chinese who lived in the neighborhood — but day-to-day existence was difficult. Against a backdrop of rapid industrialization and economic depression, the residents fought prejudice from both inside and outside the community and endured overcrowding, poor sanitation, and absentee landlords.

Railroad station

The Pennsylvania Railroad Station, on Liberty Avenue east of the Lower Hill District, was Pittsburgh's point of entry for most newcomers. Benevolent organizations such as the Centre Avenue YWCA and the Traveler's Aid Society, both within walking distance of the station, provided housing. The YWCA's Lucille Cuthbert remembers that Traveler's Aid employees would often call "to see if there was an available room for one girl or two girls who had come into the city looking for work. There was supposed to have been a policy against permanent housing, but sometimes the girl stayed there longer because she had nowhere else to go."

Progressive Era reform brought relief to some, and resentment to others. Despite the inadequacies, however, the Hill supported lively cultural and recreational activities, businesses, and religious institutions.

Extensive residential development of the Upper Hill began in 1846 when Thomas Mellon, a lawyer and founder of the Mellon banking empire, took advantage of real estate opportunities after the Great Fire of 1845. "In 1846," he writes in his autobiography, "I built some 18 small dwellings which brought me an annual income of 10% on the investment, until I sold them at a profit afterwards in 1860." The Hill's proximity to downtown made it ideal in mid-century for businessmen and their families, predominantly of Scots-Irish and German descent. The first of many out-migrations from the Hill occurred shortly after the Civil War, as the earliest streetcars helped initiate residential development four to five miles east in Oakland and Shadyside.

As this early suburbanization occurred, new arrivals, fleeing poverty, religious persecution, and mandatory and prolonged military service in their native countries, came by the tens of thousands. Between 1870 and 1920, due in part to the city's annexation of boroughs to the north and south but certainly also to mass immigration and migration, Pittsburgh's population quadrupled (139,500 to 588,500). By 1920, nearly two-thirds of the city's population were immigrants and their children. Poles and Italians began arriving in large numbers in the 1880s. So, too, with the Chinese, though the Chinese Exclusion Act of 1882 slowed the flow to a trickle. Slovaks, Syrians, Lebanese, and Galician and Rumanian Jews followed in the 1890s. In a process repeated in nearly every U.S. city, newcomers sought work, affordable housing in close proximity to work, and a helping hand through ethnic affiliations. In Pittsburgh, the masses often huddled first in the Hill.

African Americans, a constant in the Hill's diverse population, settled in the Lower Hill close to downtown as early as 1808. In that year, some established Bethel AME Church downtown, which in 1872 moved into the Hill District. Prior to the Civil War, Pittsburgh's total black population was less than 2,000, the majority living just off Wylie Avenue in an area known as "Little Hayti." The community, making up less than 5 percent of the total population and faced with racism, segregation, and low-paying jobs, still supported several churches, a school, a militia company, benevolent societies, and a temperance league. Between 1880 and 1900, the city's black population rose from 4,000 to over 20,000; social and cultural activities expanded accordingly. By

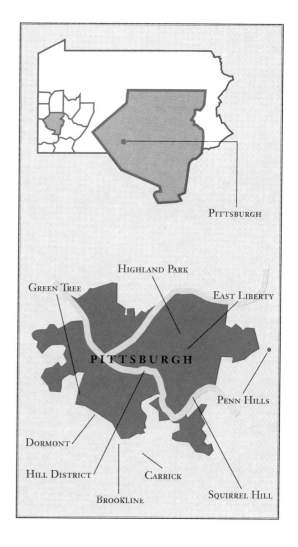

Migration advertisement

The World War I needs of America's European allies caused a massive migration of southern blacks to northern industrial cities. Ads in newspapers such as the *Pittsburgh Courier*, with a national readership of mostly African Americans, helped drive the movement. A South Carolina farmer recalls his decision to move to Pittsburgh: "I was plowin' in the field and it was real hot. And I stayed with some of the boys who would leave home and...come back...and would have money, and they had clothes. I didn't have that...And I said, 'Well, as long as I stay here I'm not going to get nowhere.' And I tied that mule to a tree and caught a train."

1900, the families of long residence were already beginning to define themselves as an elite group within the community. Within a decade, as thousands of southern black migrants arrived, many established families left the Hill for the eastern fringes of the city, where work for affluent white families could be found. Homewood became a favorite new residential spot for blacks employed as domestics, while manufacturing drew many to Greenfield-Hazelwood.

Between 1910 and 1930, drawn to jobs in Pittsburgh's vast industrial complex and to affordable housing in the Hill, 30,000 African Americans migrated to the city from the rural South. Increased production during World War I and the slowing of immigration – pinched tight after the war with the passage of the Immigration Act of 1924, which placed immigration quotas on specific countries – opened up unskilled and semi-skilled factory jobs previously closed to blacks by racist employers and company unions.

Ethnic enclaves existed within the Hill. Blacks settled most often in Ward 3, the Lower Hill around Wylie and Webster avenues. Italians, also prone to the Lower Hill, gathered close to Webster and Washington avenues. Jews and other Eastern Europeans chose the Upper Hill, Ward 5. Settlements clustered around the primary business areas frequented by the different ethnic populations. Despite the settlement patterns, census data often shows blacks and immigrants renting living space in the same buildings and frequenting a range of businesses. And remembering this ethnic crazy-quilt brings forth statements such as, "We had nice feelings. Everyone was friendly. We got along with everybody," or, "If a group of children were playing baseball and the pitcher's mother called him to go to Mass, everybody just went along, regardless of their religious affiliation, because he was going to Mass." Skin color, religion and homeland loyalties certainly created tension and conflict in this new America, but the people who coexisted in the Hill harbor overwhelmingly fond memories of life there.

Recreation and entertainment – an informal sandlot game, an after-hours jam session at the Crawford Grill, or a showdown between the Negro Baseball League's Pittsburgh Crawfords and Homestead Grays – helped bring together the diverse people of the Hill. Gus Greenlee, an African American entrepreneur and owner of the Crawford Grill, built Greenlee Field stadium in 1933. His team, the Crawfords, which had originated as an integrated neighborhood team for the city league, was permitted to play at Forbes Field but was denied use of the locker rooms and showers. The Hill was also a place where crowds, both black and white and from other neighborhoods, flocked to spend an evening in one of the nightclubs. Perhaps the most telling of statements came from a man who grew up in the Hill: "There was never an 'us and them attitude' between people on the Hill, but there were those feelings toward [people] from outside the community."

The Hill District also served as a veritable laboratory for reformers, including some previous inhabitants of the neighborhood who created organizations to benefit the health and welfare of residents. In the 1890s, just after the first wave of Polish and Italian immigrants began arriving, civic-minded, native-born Americans began an all-encompassing ("Progressive") reform movement. The Progressives sought, in general, to mold the immigrant into an "American" through instruction and better living conditions, so that the ideology and institutions of America would be a model to the world. Hill residents often speak highly of programs ranging from summer camps away from the city to public baths in the neighborhood sponsored by the Urban League of Pittsburgh, the YWCA, the YMCA, the Irene Kaufmann Settlement House, the Kingsley Settlement House, and the Wylie Avenue Branch of the Carnegie Library. Such organizations also conducted studies that resulted in calls for recreational centers, hospitals, old age homes, and homes for unwed mothers. The irony is that while these organizations sought to "Americanize" or integrate the immigrant into society, and to familiarize the migrant with northern traditions, they did so through segregation. The Irene Kaufmann Settlement predominantly served the Jewish community. Black children who wished to take music lessons at the IKS were sent to the Centre Avenue YMCA. The Kingsley Association worked only with the Italian population and in fact moved out of the Hill in the midst of the Great Migration in 1918 because of the influx of southern blacks.

However, Hill residents creatively adapted the institutional missions of the reform organizations. A study conducted in 1930 – among more than 60 written between 1900 and 1940 – found that children in the Hill spent much of their time at the Wylie Avenue branch of the Carnegie Library. However, another study complained that too many children gathered at the library and used it not for quiet study but as a social gathering space. The study's authors suggested that children need more recreational facilities. But given the large number of facilities (over 90) already available, it seems quite possible that the teens

FREE CLASSES
Learn to Read and Write English!
Pittsburgh Board of Public Education

IRENE KAUFMANN SETTLEMENT
1835 CENTER AVENUE
Monday and Wednesday 9 to 11 o'clock in the Morning
Tuesday and Thursday 1 to 3 o'clock in the Afternoon

AGUDATH ACHIM SYNAGOGUE
2919 WYLIE AVENUE
Monday and Wednesday 1 to 3 o'clock in the Afternoon

Join Now! Everybody Is Welcome!

Bring This Valuable Opportunity to the Attention of Your Relatives and Friends!
--- HAVE THEM BEGIN AT ONCE ---

(Over)

Ad for English classes
IKS and the Pittsburgh public schools offered new immigrants the chance to learn English for free. Doing so advanced two causes: English was the fast track to "Americanization," a goal of the IKS, and it improved one's capability to earn a livelihood. Joseph DiLisio, an Italian immigrant to the Hill, missed out on an education in Italy because he had to work in the fields. Arriving in Pittsburgh, he "learned the English the hard way: a little bit here and a little bit there."

found the library an escape from the formalized structure of sponsored recreation. Adults today, many of these residents recall some reform agencies as heavy-handed and demeaning in their zeal to remake newcomers into proper Americans.

Beyond social and educational programming, many organizations fought with the city for improved living conditions in the Hill. William Matthews, a Kingsley House director, battled to clear the Hill of vice and to obtain adequate housing. His complaints to the city drew little response. Matthews and Anna B. Heldman, nursing director at the IKS, turned to off-duty police detectives to document the vice, and subsequently published articles in the Kingsley House newsletter. When Matthews received no city recognition of problems associated with the inadequate, unsanitary, 19th century dwellings that dominated the Hill, he began to document them. Only with publication did attention come from the mayor. Matthews' efforts also brought Jacob Riis, a noted documentary photographer, to town. In his memoirs, Matthews asks, "What results came from all this crying out? There was much cleaning up, some tearing down, and a bit later a change in city government, with a real public health man at the head of the department."

But while Matthews had some success, the sheer number of people living in the Hill and the vast amount of work required to repair and renovate the housing meant that the reformers were never able to keep up with demand, especially during the Great Depression, when the number of people needing assistance was so enormous.

In 1930, the number of Europeans and African Americans living in the Hill District was almost even; from that point on, others moved out while blacks stayed and more arrived. For example, Jews, in general, moved further east, as far as Squirrel Hill; Italians to East Liberty, Dormont, and Penn Hills; the Lebanese to Brookline and Greentree; and Greeks and Lithuanians to the South Hills.

Lack of economic opportunity in businesses outside the neighborhood, and political coalitions detrimental to those blacks still in the Hill, left them with an increasingly stagnant community. Between 1956 and 1962, urban renewal – mainly to build the Civic Arena auditorium in the Lower Hill – displaced 2,000 families and 416 businesses. Discussion of urban renewal's encroachment into the Upper Hill, within the context of the civil rights movement of the early 1960s, brought action from a newly formed group, the Citizens Committee for Hill District Renewal. The committee worked with city planners to halt destruction of the neighborhood's remaining housing stock and to introduce anti-poverty programs in the area.

Because the Hill is such an historic city neighborhood, those perhaps not familiar with it may find a note on modern-day developments valuable. As the 20th century progressed, the Hill's multi-ethnic reputation lessened as it became almost totally an African American neighborhood. The old organizations were joined by newer reform groups, many of which focused on the problems of drug addiction and gang violence. Recent development has taken the form, especially, of new housing. In December 1992, the first residents moved into new apartments and houses in "Crawford Square." Located just above the Civic Arena between Crawford and Roberts streets, the development, in its second phase of construction by 1995, offers housing to low- and moderate-income families and individuals. Future plans include the construction of a shopping and entertainment area, in hopes of returning the Hill to its former glory, when jazz clubs were renowned and its shopping district thrived.

Johnson's deluxe market
African American-owned businesses thrived in the Hill during the 1930s and 1940s, including Johnson's, 2153 Centre Avenue. Nearly all essentials and services could be bought in the neighborhood. There were drugstores, restaurants, clubs, cleaners, barbershops, insurance agencies, funeral homes, a bank, beauty parlors, furriers, jewelers, and doctors' offices.

Destruction of the Lower Hill

Between 1956 and 1961, urban renewal in the Lower
Hill leveled nearly all old structures in the historic
neighborhood, displacing 2,000 families and individuals,
and 416 businesses. The Civic Arena was built, but a
proposed complex of luxury apartments, a museum, and
performance halls were not completed. Because 80
percent of those affected were African Americans, many
referred to the plan as "black removal" rather than urban
renewal.

1914 Hill housing

By 1910, some 51,000 people lived in the Hill District; two out of three were immigrants or the children of immigrants. African Americans numbered 10,754, while 27 nationality groups lived around them, including Poles, Italians, Russians, Ukrainians, Rumanians, Lithuanians, Hungarians, Syrians, Greeks, Czechs, South Slavs, Germans, and Irish.

Donald Jefferson in uniform (right)

Donald Jefferson, who moved as a boy with his family from Ohio to the Hill, was drafted as a freshman at the University of Pittsburgh. Military policy permitted African Americans to serve only as support personnel to white troops, with no possibility of promotion. Jefferson and other Pittsburgh soldiers' letters of complaint, most notably to *Pittsburgh Courier* publisher Robert L. Vann, led to the creation of the 351st Field Artillery unit, the first black combat unit. Jefferson, discharged as a 2nd Lieutenant, then completed his pharmacy degree at Pitt.

Traveling sharpener

"The huckster would yell, the ragman would sing, my grandfather had his bell," recalls John Antonucci, grandson of Francesco Antonucci (center). Francesco and his brother came to Pittsburgh in 1917 after hearing of plentiful work in area coal mines. Many immigrants also ran small businesses because mine pay was poor. Grinding machine in tow, Francesco Antonucci walked or rode streetcars everywhere – Braddock, Oakland, East Liberty, Highland Park – and rang a bell to attract anyone who had dull knives and scissors.

Little Lebanon

Lebanese immigrants (Lower Hill, 1940) began arriving around the turn of the century from Greater Syria. In the Hill, they established two central institutions: St. Anne's Lebanese Maronite Catholic Church and St. George's Syrian Orthodox Church. Many made a living as hucksters or peddlers. Census records from 1930 show that even after three decades, nearly 85 percent of Pittsburgh's Syrian-born immigrants lived in the Hill. Lithuanian, Greek, Mexican and Chinese immigrants also were present in the Hill.

Laying cornerstone – Holy Trinity Church

In ethnic diversity lay religious diversity as well. Early churches such as St. Brigid's and Holy Trinity, its cornerstone laid in 1894, served the Hill's early Irish and German populations respectively, two principal immigrant groups of the mid-19th century. Later congregations – Machseikei Hadas (Jewish), St. Ferdinand's (Italian), and St. Benedict the Moor (African Americans) – reflected post-1870 immigration to the Hill.

IRENE KAUFMANN SETTLEMENT STAFF-DECEMBER 1925

IKS staff photo (above)
For staff of the Irene Kaufmann Settlement (1925), pre-dominantly middle- and upper-class professionals educated during the Progressive Era, the Hill District was a laboratory for social reform. In 1921, according to one study, 93 institutions worked "to improve health, housing, education, recreation, collection of garbage, and other needs in the district."

Kingsley House brochure
"[T]he increased incidence of tuberculosis has been found to accompany the breakdown in living standards and to follow particularly closely the breakdown in housing standards." – *The Federator*

The Kingsley House, a benevolent organization located in the Hill from 1901 to 1917, offered fresh air and outdoor activities at its camp in Valencia in southern Butler County. The Hill's cramped, unsanitary conditions were a breeding ground for TB: 1,093 cases were reported in 1933 alone.

"Forget about worry, forget about money."

"Jus' happy"

IKS poster (right)

In honor of the 30th anniversary of IKS, members competed in a poster contest to highlight the goals of the settlement. Although new immigrants thought highly of Americanization, second-generation Americans such as Sydney Santmann felt it was over-emphasized. "I resented the fact that they tried to tell us how to brush our teeth and comb our hair. I was born in this country. I'm an American. And my mother was a meticulous woman. She kept us clean ... We were thankful for these people ... but there were certain elements that rubbed you the wrong way."

Anna B. Heldman (opposite page, far left in second full row)

IKS stalwart Anna B. Heldman, in her unpublished "The Neighbor's Tales" as told by "Heldie," describes how one man depicted domestic life: "'I never want to see my wife again. She is lazy and dirty and won't cook a decent meal or keep the house clean. All she does is fight with me.' Isaac was sitting in my office at the settlement, a pathetic figure. I had asked him to come to see me at the insistent request of a relative, to see if it would be possible to effect a reconciliation with his wife Hannah."

Heldman's 38 years at IKS were spent in many capacities, yet always as a "civilian rabbi," handling domestic, financial, and legal difficulties for those in need.

West Funeral Home ad fan

Thomas L. West, originally from Gordonsville, Va., lost his life savings in a bank closing, but casket companies and cemeteries loaned him money to open his funeral home in 1932. He appointed it with furniture from home. The West family still operates the business on Wylie Avenue, though it was hardly a "business" during the Depression: West became highly regarded for performing his services, even though government burial allotments often did not cover all funeral expenses.

Dry Slitz Cigar Box

Dry Slitz was the stogie brand of a Mr. Goldsmit, leader of a secret association of Hill cigar-makers called the Bosses' Association. In 1913, the group tried to smash a strike by International Workers of the World Tobacco Workers Local 101. The union sought higher wages and protested the use of child laborers. Goldsmit forbid child workers to talk on the job. The union declaration that "You smoke the blood of children if you smoke Dry Slitz" and an effective boycott significantly hurt Goldsmit's businesses by strike's end.

Lewis Hine, "Pittsburgh Stogie Maker using cutting machine," 1910 (left)

Lewis Hine, a noted documentary photographer on assignment for the Pittsburgh Survey, took this photograph at a cutting table in one of the Hill's many stogie factories. Exposing work conditions, Hine, along with Survey writer and investigator Elizabeth Beardsley Butler, fought for labor legislation especially to protect women and children. Employers insisted that smaller fingers and younger eyes worked quicker and longer – for less.

Seamstresses

Pittsburgh's garment district was in the area bounded by Smithfield Street and Sixth and Liberty avenues, within walking distance of the Hill. According to the 1930 U.S. census, 115 women from the Hill worked as seamstresses. More than 5,000 women from the Hill worked outside the home — 2,000 in domestic and personal service, almost all in prosperous neighborhoods such as Oakland, Shadyside and Squirrel Hill.

Development billboard

The first wave of destruction in the Lower Hill and the Civic Arena met with little resistance. But by 1960, debate about the future, especially about encroachment into the Upper Hill residential area, occurred in the context of a national civil rights movement. The Citizens Committee for Hill District Renewal formed in 1963. It saw additional cultural space tied to downtown corporate interests as detrimental to Hill residents. The committee also worked with city planners to introduce anti-poverty programs in the area.

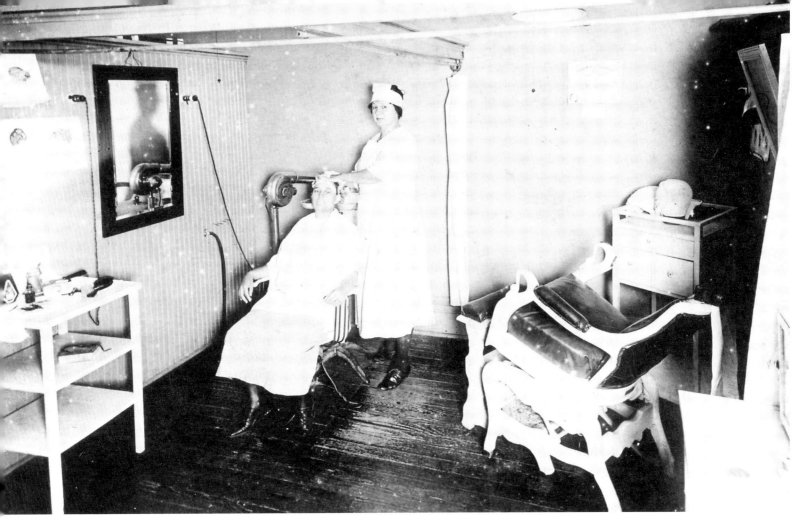

Virginia Proctor

Virginia Woodson Proctor, daughter of Pittsburgh abolitionist Lewis Woodson, lived with her children and husband above his barber shop downtown on Fourth Avenue near Market Street. When waiting wives of barber shop customers visited, Proctor took notice of their wigs and decided, in 1867, to open her own salon in the building. Eventually known for charitable work in the Hill, her business amassed a small fortune. It has been said of Proctor that she "possessed a wealth of characteristic traits that stood out like beacon lights to inspire young people to strive for the best in life." Her death in 1924 left the business in daughter Jennie's hands, in a new location on Fifth Avenue.

Courier billboard (left)

The newspaper of choice for the Hill's black residents was the *Pittsburgh Courier*. Attorney Robert L. Vann founded the paper in 1910 to compliment the activities of the NAACP and the Urban League. The paper's reform agenda included housing, education, health, job creation, politics, race relations, and crime. It featured accomplishments by notable African Americans and reports from outlying towns such as New Castle, Washington, Greensburg, Beaver Falls, and Sharon.

Candy poster

Sign posted in Machsikei Hadas Synagogue, c. 1930.

Prayer Book (far right)

St. Michael's Russian Orthodox Church (formerly a Cathedral) on Reed Street in the Hill was once the "mother" church for all Russian Orthodox congregations in the city and the seat of the diocese's bishop. Olga Krasofsky's parents lived in the Hill and met at St. Michael's. When she was 3, and part of a surging out-migration by whites to the suburbs after 1940, the family moved to the South Hills suburb of Carrick. Krasofsky and her mother returned to St. Michael's on Mother's Day 1945, when Olga received this prayer book, her first "of many more over the years ..."

Bethel Choir – 1918

Church choir (Bethel AME, 1918) and Sunday school also served social functions by offering new parishioners deeper involvement in community life. Chartered in 1818 and often referred to as "Mother Bethel," the church at Wylie Avenue and Elm Street is said to be the oldest AME church west of the Allegheny Mountains. Family matters brought Lucille Cuthbert, whose father was an AME minister in Pittsburgh, to the Hill in 1927 after two years of high school teaching in the family's hometown of Salisbury, N.C. She remembers: "I was the oldest girl, and I remember my father telling me I was needed at home to look after…the children. And I remember how lonesome I was! Oh, and I would just cry, because I didn't know any-body! You know, all I did was go to Sunday school. I still have some of those friends I met in Sunday school."

Torah Crown

This *keter Torah*, as it is known in Hebrew, crowned the scroll of the Jewish holy book in Machsekei Hadas Synagogue, Wylie Avenue and Grandville Street. Decorated with symbols, fruits, lions, and shells, the crown originally was used only on holidays, but eventually it was moved into common use. It represents honor, and among the favorite maxims of the rabbis in the *Pirke Avot* is one on the "three crowns: the crown of the Torah, the crown of the priesthood and the crown of loyalty; but the crown of good name exceeds them all."

Suggested Reading

Bachrach, Minnie Hildred, "The Immigrant on the Hill," M.A. thesis, Carnegie Institute of Technology, 1921.

Beyond Adversity, HSWP Public Programs curriculum package, 1993.

Bodnar, J., R. Simon, M. Weber, *Lives of Their Own: Blacks, Italians, and Poles in Pittsburgh, 1900-1960* (Urbana: University of Illinois Press, 1982).

Bolden, Frank, "The First Hundred Years, the Woodson-Proctor Families, 1831-," *Pittsburgh Courier*, May 13, 1950.

Chambers, Clarke A., "Toward a Redefinition of Welfare History," *Journal of American History* 73 (September 1986).

Cuthbert, Lucille, interview by Margaret Spratt, August 1992, Historical Society of Western Pennsylvania Library and Archives.

DeSimone, Josephine, interview by Catherine Cerrone and Tess Riesmeyer, August 4, 1994, HSWP Library and Archives.

Epstein, Abraham, "The Negro Migrant in the Pittsburgh," University of Pittsburgh, School of Economics, 1918.

Gottlieb, Peter, *Making Their Own Way: Southern Blacks' Migration to Pittsburgh, 1916-1930* (Urbana: University of Illinois Press, 1987).

Hays, Samuel P., ed., *City at the Point: Essays on the Social History of Pittsburgh* (Pittsburgh: University of Pittsburgh Press, 1989).

Lynch, Patrick, "Pittsburgh, the IWW and the Stogie Workers," in Conlin, Joseph R., ed., *At the Point of Production: The Local History of the IWW* (Westport, Conn.: Greenwood Press, 1981).

Mallett, William J., "Redevelopment and Response: The Lower Hill Renewal and Pittsburgh's Original Cultural District," *Pittsburgh History* 75 (Winter 1992-93).

Matthews, William A., *Adventures in Giving* (New York: Dodd, Mead and Co., 1939).

Reid, Ira A., *Social Conditions of the Negro in the Hill District of Pittsburgh* (1930).

Ruskin, Ryan S., "The Americanization of Eastern European Jewish Immigrants in Pittsburgh 1893-1920," B.A. thesis, Princeton University, 1990.

"Hill District House, Pittsburgh, Pa."
by Leonard Lieb, 1948

Woogie Harris at the Crawford Grill (right)
Woogie Harris, performing at the Crawford Grill (c. 1948), was one of the Hill's best-known businessmen and one of Pittsburgh's first African American millionaires. Denied bank loans, many blacks grew to count on Harris for business loans. Harris' Crystal Barber Shop, 1400 Wylie Avenue, was a community center of sorts – a gathering place where local news was passed along. Harris and the owner of the Crawford Grill, 1401 Wylie Avenue, promoted it as a spot to play lotto in the days before the state ran the action, and was a lively and successful restaurant and nightclub. After their downtown performances, visiting jazz greats such as Billy Eckstine, Mary Lou Williams, and Dizzy Gillespie often wandered into the Crawford Grill for sessions late into the night.

Paris Studio

Connections to the Present
Near the top of the list of infrastructure projects that created the Pittsburgh region known today is the George Westinghouse Bridge, built in 1932 in the Turtle Creek Valley. It extended the automobile's domain into suburban areas 45 miles away from Pittsburgh in Allegheny and Westmoreland counties.

CHAPTER *5*

Moving to the Suburbs

1945-1965

Essay & Captions by Gregory W. Smith

In the mid-twentieth century, Western Pennsylvania faced new challenges brought about by the combined effects of suburbanization and decentralization. The health of the regional economy was largely tied to a single industry – steel – which was subject to seasonal fluctuations and plagued by outdated technology and outmoded facilities. Like many industrial cities in the Northeast, Pittsburgh's economy boomed during World War II. After the war, suburban flight ensured that wealth gained during the war would be invested across a far wider area of the region, mostly beyond the city. Throughout its history, Pittsburgh experienced floods, fires, and labor strife. By the mid-1950s, a population drain was also underway.

Although doubts began to surface during the period about the region's longterm future, these were years of great prosperity and hope for many who lived them. This was especially true for those new and growing suburbs; there, as in the suburbs across America, the human desire for social and economic mobility combined, most obviously, with the surging technologies of the automobile industry. A new culture was born.

Suburban neighborhood

From the air, the houses in this Castle Shannon housing plan look nearly identical. They are. Modest homes built after the war, they suited a blue-collar workforce with the desire and capital to move away from the milltowns in which they worked and, often, had been born. Many became the first homeowners in their families, thanks to union wages and the G.I. Bill, which provided low-interest loans to veterans.

Previous essays in this volume have noted how industry developed in proximity to transportation routes; residential development occurred similarly. The earliest movement out of the city center occurred due to transportation innovations affordable, at first, only to the wealthiest classes, and then on a larger scale somewhat later when the same or similar forms of transportation became affordable to many. In the nineteenth century, the steam locomotive and horse-drawn streetcars carried the first waves of the upper class, then the middle class out of Pittsburgh, allowing the settlement of eastern communities such as Oakland, Shadyside and Wilkinsburg. In 1871, the first streetcars ventured into the South Hills, often bound for parks and amusements owned or promoted by streetcar and transit companies. These lines prepared the territory for the primary post-World War II suburban expansion.[1] By the beginning of the 20th century, streetcar lines were also factors in the growth of industrial centers on the Pittsburgh fringe, such as Homestead, especially in the residential areas favored by local company managers.

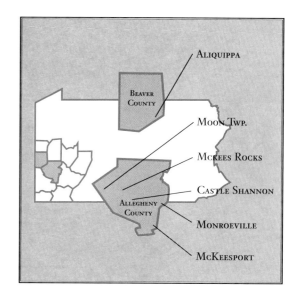

Early 20th century real estate broadsides reveal the variety of living situations afforded Western Pennsylvanians. The King Place plan, on the back of Mt. Washington, for example, was touted as an escape from the crowding and perceived unhealthiness of city life. Unmentioned in the broadside, but no doubt a factor in individual desires to leave the city, were the waves of Eastern and Southern European immigrants who saturated the region (and concentrated in the city) during the first two decades of the century. Although developments such as King House Plan were located on the outskirts of the city, its residents – of mainly northern European descent whose families had come in the nineteenth century – depended on streetcar lines to travel to and from work in the Golden Triangle.

Since the appearance of independent mill towns in the late 19th century, a large portion of Allegheny County residents have lived outside Pittsburgh's city limits. Automobiles accelerated the push out, in the mill towns and in Pittsburgh. Only the wealthiest families owned automobiles in first decades of the century. By the 1920s, mass production had reduced the cost of cars significantly, making them affordable to the middle class. Access to cars increased the rate of suburban flight, as well as the distance suburbanites could travel to work, entertainment and shopping. In 1924, when the Liberty Tunnels breached the barrier of Mt. Washington into the South Hills, a large

Liberty Tubes postcard

The Liberty Tunnels – called the "Tubes" – was the first automobile tunnel in the country when it punctured the barrier of Mt. Washington above the South Side in 1924. This postcard image shows the tunnel's northern mouth (with a traffic circle later removed) on the Liberty Bridge. South Hills suburbs, easily reached via the tunnel, grew dramatically in the years after the Tubes opened. The population of Mt. Lebanon, for example, increased nearly five-fold between 1920 and 1930 (2,258 to 13,403).

segment of Pittsburgh's middle class flooded through. The population of communities on the southern end of the tunnels exploded in the 1920s due to the opening, while the population of many communities bypassed by the Tubes stagnated.[2] As late as 1934, however, only about 20 percent of Pittsburgh residents drove to work, while nearly half still depended on streetcars, and another third walked. Over three-fourths of residents in Monongahela Valley mill towns walked to work. Working-class access to cars in the postwar period would soon change that pattern.[3]

At the turn of the 20th century, new industrial towns and old towns rejuvenated by industrial jobs, such as McKeesport, dotted the region's map. Land developers created housing plans to attract workers, and upscale housing catering to the managers, businessmen, and shop owners who thrived on the booming economy. Real estate developers in towns such as Munhall and Turtle Creek touted each as the city of the future. Many advertising broadsides appealed to the upwardly mobile aspirations of the middle class. (One claimed Trafford as the "Sewickley of the Westinghouse Valley.") In each case, proximity to industrial facilities was considered advantageous. Real estate promoters in McKeesport extolled the virtues of the massive steel pipe works nearby. Many advertisements featured industrial facilities in the foreground, at a time when oversized factories symbolized economic prosperity. Still, many industrial workers and their families had to settle for the courts and tenements literally in the shadow of mills, as described by Margaret Byington in the *Pittsburgh Survey* of 1907.

The Depression and World War II interrupted the suburban

expansion, but events during the 1930s and '40s spurred new approaches to housing and development. Sponsored by the Buhl Foundation, Chatham Village on Mt. Washington was a particularly successful attempt to create planned housing for moderate-income families. It was, however, the exception. In the city, urban renewal through demolition greatly reduced the percentage of substandard units, but government showed less concern for alternatives. In 1938, the Housing Authority of Pittsburgh constructed the low-income Bedford Dwellings and Addison Terrace, but all subsequent projects built through 1945 gave preference to the families of those working in the armaments industry. Generally excluded were the original federal targets for public housing – marginally or unemployed workers, mostly racial minorities. By the end of the war, despite the desire of the Housing Authority to keep the housing racially mixed, an African American presence in PHA projects was reciprocated by an exodus of white residents.[4]

There are many reasons for the dramatic growth of postwar suburbs. More people could afford to purchase homes than ever before. World War II brought the federal armaments dollars to the region that pulled the region's economy up by its bootstraps. Steel, aluminum, and glass, along with all types of heavy machinery including ships, jeeps and airplanes, were produced locally.[5] The increased capacity of the mills prepared the region for the industrial boom of the 1950s, when millions of tons of steel were needed for bridge and building construction, consumer durables, and a Pentagon budget bloated by the Korean War and the Cold War.

Other federal programs set the stage for increased suburbanization as well. In 1944, the work of the Federal Housing Administration was supplemented by the Serviceman's Readjustment Act (the G.I. Bill), designed to help 16 million World War II veterans purchase homes and attend school. The G.I. Bill called for long-term, government-backed mortgages by private lenders, requiring only small down-payments (usually less than 10 percent). Due to this and other federal programs, purchasing a house was cheaper than renting.[6]

The G.I. Bill also entitled veterans to attend college free of charge. Those who had served for three years earned the right to attend four years at any accredited college, university, trade school, professional school, or even high school or elementary school. The G.I. Bill made a significant impact on Western Pennsylvania by offering veterans a choice where none had existed before. Many chose to attend the

Ann McCastland, Westinghouse, E. Pittsburgh
Working women in Western Pennsylvania generally were limited to white collar positions such as teachers and clerks. But during World War II, Pittsburgh's industrial plants offered women war work at good wages. Ann McCastland, a Miami, Fla. model, responded to a plea for employees at the East Pittsburgh plant of Westinghouse Electrical and Manufacturing Co. "I could be helping out my husband, who is in the Marines, as well as myself," she explained. After the war, returning soldiers displaced most female industrial workers, who left the workforce or returned to lower-status, lower-paid positions.

Home front banner

Objects and mementos from the wartime home front include those honoring family members serving overseas. Banners with gold stars displayed in windows identified households with family members killed in action. The Perrot family had a banner in their North Side home. It had blue stars. All three of their sons returned home safely.

University of Pittsburgh, the largest institution of higher learning in the region. In the fall of 1946, 83 percent of the male undergraduates were veterans, mostly enrolled in engineering and business classes. In 1948, the *New York Times* reported that Pitt had the 10th largest veteran enrollment in the nation.

The G.I. bill did not drain the region of blue-collar workers, though. The region had an exceptionally low proportion of high school seniors continuing on to college, opting instead for trade schools, apprenticeships, or jobs in industry. The collective bargaining powers afforded to labor unions under the Wagner Act (1935) led to the upward economic mobility of blue collar workers. By the 1940s, steel and other large-scale industries were nearly 100 percent unionized, and American steelworkers were among the highest paid industrial workers in the world. The spending power of blue collar families allowed many to own cars and boats, as well as homes.[7]

Middle-class automobile ownership became common. In 1949, 50,000 cars were sold in Allegheny County – a record to that date. New federal infrastructure programs such as the Interstate Highway Act of 1956 stimulated highway construction across America. Pittsburgh-area communities and the state built miles of new roads, bridges and tunnels. The Penn-Lincoln Parkway cut across the county, becoming a major commuter route to downtown jobs and bringing the new airport in Moon Township within reach of dozens of new boroughs. Monroeville, in eastern Allegheny County, grew dramatically when the Turnpike reached it and again when the Parkway was completed, attracting the middle class from Pittsburgh and Westinghouse workers from Turtle Creek Valley towns. Monroeville, known for the shopping centers along its "Miracle Mile," became synonymous with "suburb" in the minds of Western Pennsylvanians.

The Pittsburgh area is practically distinct among U.S. metropolitan areas for its many independent boroughs and school districts. Some suburbs are oriented towards Pittsburgh; their residents work in the city, and depend on it for shopping and entertainment. Then there are the industrial mill towns, and still other suburbs oriented toward them. Before the war, working men of West Mifflin, for example, usually commuted to industrial facilities in Homestead, Duquesne or McKeesport. They may have travelled to Pittsburgh to shop or see a show on special occasions, but for the most part, at least until the 1970s, the mill towns could support a mixture of local businesses. Such towns also remained the social hub of blue-collar families, where people worshipped, shopped, and socialized. This changed as suburban residents built such institutions closer to home. Suburban shopping centers decimated many mill town business districts after the 1970s.

Middle-class African American families moved to suburbs as well, but in lower proportions, and to a limited number of communities (Penn Hills being among the most prominent, though not until the late 1970s). Left behind was an isolated underclass in Pittsburgh neighborhoods such as the Hill, Beltzhoover, Larimer, and Homewood-Brushton, especially after urban renewal in Pittsburgh's Lower Hill District forced mass relocations to affordable housing in older neighborhoods of the city's fringes.

Advances in communication and transportation facilitated intermingling of children of immigrants, who shared many aspects of pop culture through radio and television. While suburbs often mirrored the segregated nature of city neighborhoods, ethnicity played a decreasing role, often revealed only through choice of church, and (diminishingly) through ethnic clubs or fraternals, schools, and events such as Kennywood Park's "ethnic days." New generations, not surprisingly, were less likely to identify themselves ethnically, as increasing intermarriage created children of mixed ethnicity.

Post-war Pittsburgh was, and still is, a fragmented metropolis. The city's population peaked in 1950 at 676,806 (marginally higher than 1940), then began a precipitous decline. The population of Allegheny County, however, continued to grow into the 1960s, indicating that a substantial number of families leaving Pittsburgh were settling in nearby low-density suburbs. The suburbanization of the mid-century left Western Pennsylvania even more fragmented, and less prepared to face the challenges that the deindustrialization of the 1980s would bring.

Swift Home brochure & home model
Swift Homes, founded in 1949 in Elizabeth, was the largest pre-cut wood house producer in the world. Swift salesmen nationwide carried miniature cardboard models to show the variety of house styles available. Swift homes were sold as components, to be assembled on the purchasers' lot in just a few days. Sales were strong in the Pittsburgh area.

Two suburbs

Pleasant Hills and West Mifflin offer a good comparison between white-collar and blue-collar South Hills suburbs. Although they are adjacent to each other, they are examples of two distinct suburb types: the white color commuter suburb and the working-class suburb. Each has different orientations toward Pittsburgh, different income and education levels, and ethnic proportions, but they still show many characteristics of the larger postwar suburbanization pattern.

West Mifflin, situated at a bend in the Monongahela River and surrounded by the industrial towns of Duquesne, Homestead, McKeesport, Dravosburg, and Clairton, quickly became a blue-collar suburb. An article from the 1951 *Pittsburgh Press* series on the growth of Pittsburgh suburbs characterized West Mifflin as a "fat lady in suburban dress," and a "working-man's heaven." Home of the Allegheny County Airport (Pittsburgh's primary airport until 1953), and numerous large industries, including the U.S. Steel Irvin Works, West Mifflin industry employed 13,000 in 1950. About 79 percent of employed men worked in blue-collar positions, and averaged nine years of education. West Mifflin's population doubled to nearly 18,000 during the 1940s, partly due to mill expansion in nearby Homestead, but also because many new housing plans were constructed after the war. The River View Homes war workers project was among the earliest residences on the bluff. Postwar house development was swift, with dwelling units increasing from 2,080 to 4,864 between

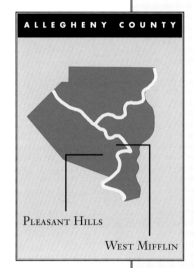

ALLEGHENY COUNTY

PLEASANT HILLS

WEST MIFFLIN

1940 and 1950. Many families bought the first home that became available to them because construction could not keep up with demand. Many new couples stayed with families until separate housing could be found. Alberts Construction built four large suburban plans in the late 1940s and early 1950s, featuring nearly identical modest homes.

In the 1950s, West Mifflin residents looked to nearby industrial towns for shopping, churches, and entertainment. Public transportation was limited — access to downtown Pittsburgh via streetcar required at least two transfers, but trolley lines ran directly to Duquesne and McKeesport, where most residents did their shopping. The Duquesne Village shopping center was built in 1959 on a West Mifflin slag dump. Residents could also frequent several movie theaters in McKeesport. Although two Catholic churches were built in West Mifflin by 1958 (along with seven Protestant), most residents attended their former ethnic-oriented churches in the mill towns.

Pleasant Hills, adjacent to lower West Mifflin near a U.S. Steel-owned slag dumping ground, took off as a middle-class white-collar suburb after the war, with housing stock doubling in the years between 1947 and 1957. At 3 square miles, it is less than one-fifth the size of West Mifflin. "Despite its nearness to a big slag pile, the community has developed into an area of pleasant homes and streets," noted the *Pittsburgh Press*. Pleasant Hills became a borough in 1948, after declaring independence from the largely undeveloped Jefferson Borough. With no manufacturing facilities, Pleasant Hills served as a bedroom community for the city of Pittsburgh, and for professionals working in local industry. Two-thirds of employed men in Pleasant Hills held white-collar positions, roughly the same proportion of blue-collar workers in West Mifflin. The annual median income in 1950 was higher than that of West Mifflin ($5,542 compared to $3,292), and nearly twice the median income of Pittsburgh. The borough also had a higher percentage of college graduates than West Mifflin, and a median education level of 12.5 years. Affluence was by no means conspicuous in Pleasant Hills, though, with no incomes over $10,000 reported in 1950. Working women in both Pleasant Hills' and West Mifflin's households were about 19 percent, mostly in sales or clerical positions. A single non-white family lived in Pleasant Hills in 1960, compared with 343 in West Mifflin. Houses in Pleasant Hills were generally $5,000-10,000 more expensive than those in West Mifflin.

Pleasant Hills was much more reliant on automobiles than West Mifflin. Public transportation in Pleasant Hills was limited, with infrequent buses to Pittsburgh and no streetcar lines. One woman interviewed in 1993 complained about the early days in her new house at the end of a dirt road, with no way to get to the shopping center. The Bill Green Shopping Plaza, built in 1949 on the first cloverleaf interchange in the state, served the immediate community. Two of the most popular nightclubs in the county -— Bill Green's and the Ankara — were located in the borough.

Both communities had high fertility ratios in the 1960 census, with Pleasant Hills reporting a ratio of children under 5 to women of child-bearing age some 200 points over the ratio in the metropolitan area. In West Mifflin, the postwar baby boom resulted in overcrowded classrooms, with 2,900 students in grade and junior high schools. By 1958, West Mifflin had two high schools, three junior highs, and seven elementary schools. In 1960, some 4,000 children aged 7 to 13 enrolled in West Mifflin schools.

Twenty years later, Century III Mall would reshape another slag dump, this one on the two boroughs' borders. Today, the mall and its attendant development are a big draw for workers and shoppers from both suburbs.

King Place Plan

A predecessor of the postwar suburban housing boom was King Place, an early 20th century middle-class plan on the southern down-slope of Mt. Washington. Access was easy by rail to the Golden Triangle, but the city's smoke, crime and crowding were absent. Compared to suburban areas in the East End, promoters argued, the natural barrier of Mt. Washington shielded King Place from the "demon Smoke" of "murky" Pittsburgh. In short time, though, the open space around such developments was wall-to-wall housing.

Parade of steel products

J & L Steel hoped to counteract the increasing use of steel substitutes, such as aluminum and plastic, with 1950s advertising campaigns. Elaborate photo shoots within and around J & L facilities showed steel's impact on American consumers. One such event was a parade of people and steel products on a bluff above J & L's Aliquippa Works, in Beaver County. Changing the image of the large and seemingly impersonal industry to that of a gentle giant was one goal; sympathy for increased tarriffs on imported steel was another.

Overflowing with Hredzaks

The Hredzak children (L to R: Mark, John, cousin Tom Delsandro, Joe, with sister Marianne barely visible behind Mark) belong to the "Baby Boom" generation. Their father, John, grew up in the industrial town of Donora, Washington County, while McKees Rocks was their mother Marie's hometown. The family settled in Castle Shannon in 1954. The children, born in rapid succession over the next six years, attained a middle-class lifestyle barely imaginable to their immigrant grandparents.

George & Lori Gatto

Family albums since the 1950s usually contain many people/car pictures. George and Lori Gatto grabbed their dog Champ for a family portrait with their 1954 Ford in Arnold. Automobiles, once considered luxuries, within only a few decades had become necessities treated as "one of the family." They also delivered a cultural revolution of sorts — coinciding with the emergence of a distinct auto-borne teenage culture — of shopping centers and subdivisions negotiated most easily, most conveniently, by car.

"Spring in the Mon Valley"
by Marty Cornelius
In 1947, Pittsburgher Marty Cornelius picked a vantage point on the South Side slopes for her painting. Hoping to "capture the mood of the city in my time," hers is a mosaic of serene working-class houses on a background of industry. Neither the Jones & Laughlin steel mill nor the Duquesne Brewery, shown prominently here, operate today.

"Teaching by Television"
The wonder of television in the 1950s led to hope for it advancing education. Pittsburgh's WQED, the nation's first public station (1954), was a national leader in children's programming, and Fred "Mister Rogers" its best-known advocate and personality.

High school students tour ET works
U.S. Steel's "Visiting Days" for seniors, such as these fellows from Scott High School (May 1955), was a means to recruit future steelworkers and acquaint them with the mill's operations. William E. Crouch, general superintendent of the Edgar Thomson Works in Braddock, showed the boys around. Despite the huge number of local veterans who attended college on the G.I. Bill after World War II, union wages and job security in a steel job remained a viable alternative.

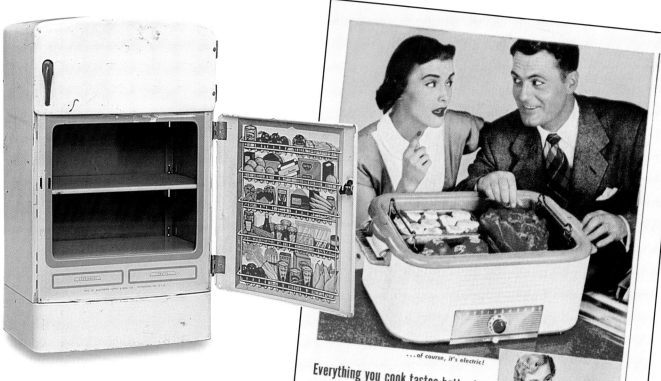

Wolverine refrigerator

Although Pittsburgh's economy was dominated by heavy industry, several smaller companies, such as Wolverine Manufacturing Co., produced consumer goods in the area. Its line of toy appliances was simple, yet charming. A metal kitchen set, its best-known product, included a sink, stove and refrigerator. Wolverine, originally located on the present site of Three Rivers Stadium, moved to Arkansas in 1970.

Westinghouse Roaster advertisement

Women infatuated with new household appliances were a common post-war ad pitch. Western Pennsylvanians maintained loyalty to Westinghouse – founded in Pittsburgh in 1870, the company was always headquartered here – although appliances such as the popular roaster were manufactured elsewhere.

. . . of course, it's electric!

Everything you cook tastes better in

America's Leading Roaster

Westinghouse ROASTER-OVEN

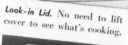

Look-in Lid. No need to lift cover to see what's cooking.

"Never knew how grand my cakes could be" . . . "how marvelous a steak could taste" . . . "how golden-brown and juicy a turkey could come out." That's what a million women say about the out-of-this-world cooking magic of this versatile Westinghouse Roaster-Oven.

You can pop in a roast and never give it a second look . . . no basting, no watching. Bakes pies, cakes, *any* kind of pastry to perfection, *every* time. Cook a complete meal for 8 or 10 with equal ease. It's the accurate thermostat control that does it.

With the detachable Broiler-Grid, you can broil, grill, fry, toast . . . anything and everything. Yes, this wonder-cooking appliance gives you all the clean, cool, work-saving sureness of electric cooking in only 2 sq. ft. of space. Give one to yourself . . . and to your favorite someone. See your nearby Westinghouse retailer today. The Westinghouse Electric Corporation, Electric Appliance Division. Mansfield, O.

Extra Capacity for large turkeys, using inset pan as cover.

Convenient Cabinet and Timer, also Broiler-Grid, are optional.

See TV's Top Dramatic Show . . . "Westinghouse STUDIO ONE" . . . Every Week

YOU CAN BE SURE..IF IT'S **Westinghouse**

Mixer   Coffee Maker   Iron   Electric Comforter   Griddle   Waffle Bakes   Toaster

86

Ethnic days, c. 1960

Kennywood, in West Mifflin, is an amusement park, but more importantly, Kennywood is a gathering place. Schools, businesses and ethnic groups continue to sponsor special days at Kennywood, as they did a century ago. Ethnic populations, dispersed throughout the region when solid urban communities fled to the suburbs, use these "nationality days" as a means to share in their heritage.

Kennywood sign

Signs pointing the way to Kennywood are as much a part of the Pittsburgh landscape as the amusement park itself. Located along the Monongahela River, Kennywood originated as a "trolley park" in the 1890s to promote streetcar ridership. By the 1950s, it had developed into a full-scale amusement park and a local cultural icon. Metal "finger pointing" Kennywood signs are rare, having been replaced in the 1960s with a simpler "arrow" design.

Eat'n Park

Former Isaly's dairy company executive Larry Hatch opened his first Eat'n Park in 1949 on Saw Mill Run Boulevard in the South Hills. Like local chains across the country, Eat'n Parks opened mainly on busy suburban commercial strips – with ample parking, which eateries in older sections of Pittsburgh could not match. Eat'n Park survived, even after the novelty of early carhop service wore off, to become the area's favorite restaurant chain.

Endnotes

[1] Toker, Franklin, *Pittsburgh: An Urban Portrait* (State College, Pa.: Penn State University Press, 1986), 280.

[2] Hoffman, Steven J., "The Saga of the Liberty Tubes: Geographical Partisanship on the Urban Fringe," *Pittsburgh History* 75, No. 3 (Fall 1992): 128-141.

[3] Lind, Aulis O., "Research Letter," *Pittsburgh Area Transportation Study*, Jan.-Feb. 1961, 5.

[4] Brown, Robert K., *Public Housing in Action: the Record of Pittsburgh* (Pittsburgh: University of Pittsburgh Press, 1959), 22-46.

[5] Harper, Frank C., *Men and Women of Wartime Pittsburgh and Environs: A War-production Epic* (published by author, 1945).

[6] Jackson, Kenneth, *Crabgrass Frontier* (New York: Oxford University Press, 1985), 206-08.

[7] Oestreicher, Richard, "Working-class Formation, Development, and Consciousness in Pittsburgh, 1790-1960," in S. Hays, ed., *City at the Point* (Pittsburgh: University of Pittsburgh Press, 1989), 142.

**Highland Park Pool after desegregation —
Photograph by Teenie Harris**

Defacto segregation remained common into the 1950s. Barriers to interracial dating and socializing were among the most difficult to overcome. In 1951, when a group of white teenagers ejected Urban League executive Joe Allen from the Highland Park Pool, the NAACP filed, and won, a suit against the City of Pittsburgh for failure to maintain safe conditions at public facilities. The struggle to desegregate the pool is still viewed as a highlight of Pittsburgh's civil rights movement.

"The 'private pool administration' of hoodlums at the Highland Park Swimming Pool, which has for years limited the use of these city-owned facilities to whites only, has gone to the well once too often..."

— *Pittsburgh Courier*, 30 June 1951

CHAPTER 6

After the Renaissance

1965-1995

Essay by Michelle Fanzo & Captions by Gregory Smith

More than 125 years have passed since the national press deemed Pittsburgh "Hell with the lid off," and 50 years have passed since it was internationally recognized as the steel producing capital of the world. Now, Big Steel is as much a part of the city's past as William Pitt, Duke beer and Forbes Field. The smoke has left the smoky city, abandoned steel sites are being adapted to new uses, and many former steelworkers have retired or retrained and continue to work and live in the region. From H. L. Mencken's 1920s assessment that Pittsburgh was a place "so dreadfully hideous, so intolerably bleak and forlorn that to reduce the whole aspiration of man to a macabre and depressing joke," to Rand McNally's 1985 christening of the former steel capital as America's "most livable city," Pittsburgh has become a showpiece of urban rebirth.

Or so it seemed ten years ago. In 1996, a decade after the worst mill layoffs in the city's history, "downsizing" and fallout from merger activity among its corporations continue to claim scores of high-paying manager jobs. Since Rand McNally decided Pittsburgh was *the* place to live, the city has lost half of its Fortune 500 companies.

"Sun Bath Tat is Hot"
(previous page)
By Anthony DeBernardin, 1965

Gateway buildings
The Renaissance called for redevelopment of an operating business district in the Golden Triangle. During the condemnation proceedings that made way for the glittering Gateway Center office complex, small business owners argued their properties did not contribute to blight; they insisted that civic improvement benefitted a few corporations, not the larger community. The state courts sided with redevelopers.

In addition, the city has a poor record in the business sectors other cities relied on in the '80s and early '90s. The situation leaves most of those people urging patience during Pittsburgh's "transition" unable to answer "Transition to what?" Others believe an attractive Phoenix rose from the ashes of the steel industry but that in today's globally competitive economy, just showing up is not enough.

While much has happened in the city's history since 1965, a logical focus for those still around (and in this essay) is what has happened in the last 20 years to the livelihoods of so many friends and family members. At the dawn of America's third century, there is reason for grave concern that Pittsburgh cannot participate — economically at least — at the high level its residents were accustomed to in the past.

Some of the reasons for the concern:

- While many former steelworkers still live in Pittsburgh, and some metals and coke are still produced in the area, the city lost half its population over the last four decades and continues to lose many of its young people to opportunities in other regions. A bit more than 12 percent of the population moved on between 1970 and 1990 alone, the highest relative decline of any U.S. urban area. Those who remain give Pittsburgh's population a retirement community profile, with 17 percent of its residents over 65, barely behind Miami as the country's oldest mean urban population.

- Expansion in the high technology and service sectors has failed to compensate for the loss of manufacturing, and metropolitan Pittsburgh's service sector can claim the slowest growth rate in the country.

- Pittsburgh ranks near the bottom of metro areas in key indicators of economic health. It has the lowest median personal income of the nation's 25 largest cities. It is viewed as having chronic labor problems, and has one of the highest net corporate income taxes. In addition, while antiquated laws and regulations — many are state statutes, the responsibility of Pennsylvania legislators — are said to hinder the competitiveness of local companies, communication and resolve among organizations promoting regional growth is no less confused and uncoordinated.

- Concerns are growing about the area's ability to support its cultural institutions and pay for municipal services, even after Allegheny County adopted a 1 percent "regional assets" sales tax in 1994. Much of the city's aging infrastructure is dilapidated, and

Pa Pitt & clean-up kids

A public campaign to "clean-up, fix-up, paint-up" encouraged Pittsburgh residents to help beautify their city by improving their homes and communities. School groups participated by sprucing up vacant lots. Sometimes, Pa Pitt, a pseudo-historical figure representing Pittsburgh's early days as a military outpost, supervised (c. 1952). "Pa" reached the height of popularity during Pittsburgh's 1958 bicentennial.

Donora & smoke

Despite the adage that smoke means prosperity, industrial pollutants are also deadly. In October 1948, 23 people in Donora, Washington County, died after mill pollution and smog hung over the town in the heavily industrialized Monongahela Valley for nearly a week. This photo, taken less than six months after the "Donora Inversion," reveals the degree to which a community could suffer in return for economic stability.

modern highways and transit routes are as fragmented and isolated as the political landscape they traverse.

Attitudes and expectations inherited over generations of omnipresent industry, however, cannot fade as quickly as the mills themselves. Pittsburgh was built, and for over a century sustained, on a single premise: that industry would provide jobs. If an individual worked hard, there would be opportunity, with family and community present to help if tough times arose. Strikes, worker discontent, company loyalty, corporate civic involvement — these were all part of the system, good or bad. Local government and individuals alike took cues about whatever future could be imagined from the big companies that paid the taxes and held the jobs upon which communities depended. When that system suddenly disappeared, the human parts of the machinery were the least equipped for change.

Some say Pittsburgh's current setbacks are mainly a reflection of national urban problems, and in that context, Pittsburgh faces fewer afflictions than many of its peers. They suggest the city needs more time for new revitalization initiatives to produce results. In its favor, Pittsburgh has had a number of years to work on its rebirth.

While the extent of the region's commercial decline was unmistakable by the mid-1980s, the city had begun a significant transformation away from its smoky image as early as the late 1940s. At that time, civic leaders such as Mayor David Lawrence and financier Richard King Mellon joined forces with many of the city's corporate and civic leaders to initiate a $500 million Renaissance I, one of the nation's first urban makeovers. Painstaking elimination of downtown blight, extending as far east as the Lower Hill District, and environmental cleanup, including strict controls on coal as a heating fuel, made Pittsburgh a trendsetter. A second urban renewal program, the $4.5 billion Renaissance II, continued the process in the late 1970s under the guidance of Mayor Richard Caliguiri.

That corporate leaders and average citizens alike in Pittsburgh have shown, time and again, a willingness to bounce back from adversity is universally appreciated. Pittsburghers pride themselves in an underlying gumption, a tenacious human spirit, that cannot be measured on charts and graphs. "I love this city," says Mike Pruszynski, a former Heppenstahl Co. steelworker who lives in the Lawrenceville section of the city. "I've been to other places — two years in New York, 38 months in the service — but I always knew I'd come back here. And

David Lawrence & acetylene torch

David L. Lawrence was mayor of Pittsburgh from 1946 to 1959, and later a U.S. senator. Although corporate leaders initiated the projects in the Pittsburgh Renaissance, political approval belonged to Lawrence, who proved to be a popular public face for the Allegheny Conference and its often controversial initiatives. Lawrence is shown handling an acetylene torch at an event celebrating the construction of Fort Duquesne Boulevard (c. 1954).

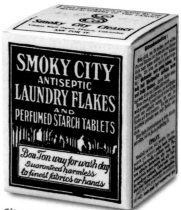

Smoky City soap

In the 20th century, local manufacturers tried to capitalize on Pittsburgh's notoriety as a filthy place to live and work. The implicit message in the packaging of "Smoky City" soap is the product's ability to perform in the worst of environments, where white shirts became dirty on the way to the office. By the late 1940s, civic leaders were trying to halt unchecked polluting.

Smoky downtown (right)

Dense smoke that turned day into night, tangled wires of overhead streetcar lines, and poorly maintained roads contributed to Pittsburgh's tired appearance in the mid-twentieth century. The Golden Triangle remained hidden under layers of grime, which Renaissance promoters sought to wipe away through smoke control and a massive clean-up program.

I'm not going to leave. I like everything about this city, even though it's gone through some hard times. In Pittsburgh, if something's not working, people try to change it. They stick together and work hard."

Hard work is what propelled Pittsburgh to emerge from World War II as an undisputed industrial powerhouse. Sure the place looked like hell (literally), but its ethic embodied the indomitable American spirit recognized and respected internationally. Pittsburgh was know-how, ingenuity, opportunity, sweat, baseball, apple pie, Klondike bars. "The place was a machine," recalls Denis Colwell, Music Director of the River City Brass Band. "You could stand on one of the city's hills and watch smoke just pouring out of dozens of mills. It was powerful. There was a sense, all the way into the 1970s, that absolutely *anything* could be done in Pittsburgh."

Pride and financial success in the postwar era — extended by an upturn during the Vietnam War — helped mask nagging structural problems in the steel industry. Some say the industry's demise began with the 1959 steel strike, when 150,000 Pittsburghers walked off the job. Others point to surging Japanese, Korean and Brazilian steel production in the 1960s, or to the lack of shop-floor worker participation in company decision-making throughout the 1970s. But clearly some of the most debilitating actions were decisions, as early as the 1920s, to limit investment in modernization. The mills were producing well. Pittsburgh had the best steel in the world. World War II erupted and the city assumed mythic status, producing 40 percent of the nation's steel. Why spend a lot of money on new equipment and infrastructure when you are already number one?

This refusal to keep up with technical innovation, many observers point out, continued to haunt the region after the war as well. Pittsburgh's mills were numerous and productive, but they also required far more "man-hours" to make a ton of steel than new mills built elsewhere in the world. The region had lost its competitive edge.

"It was pretty obvious to anyone coming to Homestead in the late '70s and looking at the quality of equipment, or going to Youngstown and seeing steam engines still powering rolling mills, that something was drastically wrong," union worker-turned-analyst Charles McCollester, who now teaches in the labor relations department at Indiana University of Pennsylvania, explained in a 1990 presentation at the Historical Society of Western Pennsylvania. Steel manufacturing jobs had gone from 150,000 in the 1950s to less than 50,000 by the early 1980s, and to 20,000 by 1989. Today less than 4 percent of the

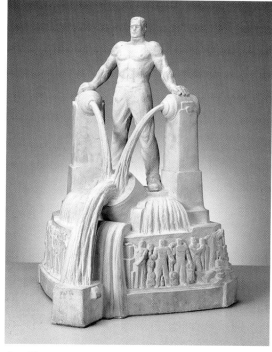

Joe Magarac

Pittsburgh sculptor Frank Vittor proposed that a giant statue of Joe Magarac, a mythical steelworker akin to Paul Bunyan, be placed downtown at the Point. In late 1950s, the Allegheny Conference on Community Development, the corporate leadership for Pittsburgh's post-World War II Renaissance, rejected Vittor's vision in favor of a more benign fountain. Perhaps to those who would shape the region's future, Joe Magarac, said to squeeze hot metal into rails, symbolized an era already past.

region's workers make primary metals and less than 12 percent work in manufacturing of any kind. So when did the reality of the end of steel sink in?

"It still hasn't for some people," says August Carlino, executive director of the Steel Industry Heritage Corporation in Homestead. "I've talked to folks who still believe that the industry can be recovered here — but as the mills have come down, this hope is less likely. As long as the mills stand, as long as a shed remains, there will still be a hope by some people that they can be reopened. But the region can never be the way it was. New mills would be so highly mechanized that they would demand a more skilled workforce and employ far fewer people than in the past."

As steel companies pulled out, unemployment was at an all time high (14.7 percent in 1983). Much of the city's most visible real estate was contaminated with industrial pollutants and people left Pittsburgh in droves, many for the South and Southwest. The impact was so staggering that many residents rejected the facts laid before them. For up to a year, workers stood outside the gates of the Jones and Laughlin steel mill in Lawrenceville, lunch pails in hand, waiting for the gates to reopen. Not only were their jobs gone, so was their sense of identity and self-worth. These are characteristics that the city is still struggling to redefine today.

Remembering & Rethinking Pittsburgh

The steel decline does not account for all contemporary changes in Pittsburgh. Large-scale suburbanization worsened the decline of many blue-collar Pittsburgh neighborhoods in the early 1960s. Moving to towns like Penn Hills, Shaler or Oakmont meant a chance to own a home or, perhaps, to escape an overly attentive family. In the city, communities like Garfield and Manchester met a triple-whammy of suburban allure, economic downturn, and problems in extensive public housing tracts that drove people from their homes. Commercial districts began to collapse and neighborhood demographics changed significantly, further polarizing those who remained. An increasing loss of community stability, which some say began with the break up of the Hill District during Renaissance I, also gained steam in the private sector.

"Until the 1980s, there were significant community ties between corporations, banks and heavy industry in Pittsburgh, and they were all doing relatively well," explains Sandra Williamson, professor of economics at the University of Pittsburgh. "Corporations supported community programs and cultural activities. Now CEOs of almost all the major corporations and foundations in the area are not from the region and this, combined with tighter pocketbooks and more emphasis on the bottom line, has diminished the essence of civic responsibility that used to be such an integral part of Pittsburgh."

However, few cities have ever been blessed with the level of civic-mindedness expressed by Pittsburgh's corporate community. While corporations may be giving less today than in the past, the private sector's civic commitment is still the envy of many other regions. Pittsburgh's corporations and foundations have proven an effective retaining wall against a greater level of urban degeneration. Downtown Pittsburgh did not experience the virtual shutdown suffered, for instance, by Akron, Cleveland, and Youngstown, in great part because of continued private sector investment in the district. At the same time, Pittsburgh's foundations have quietly amassed assets that make the city's foundation sector among the most important in the country. The Richard King Mellon Foundation, with over $1 billion in assets, is now the country's 18th largest and the Heinz Endowment is the 43rd largest.

On a different front, the influence of transportation has been significant during every period of the city's history (as many of the essays in this book point out). Most recently, suburbanization and the car culture it spawned have generated critical problems associated with economic growth in Pittsburgh: choking lines of traffic and limited accessibility. The new $700 million airport offers excellent connections to the rest of the world, but there is no mass transit link to the city, subjecting residents and visitors alike to the horse-coach speed of the jammed Parkway at busy hours. Other areas, such as the Monongahela Valley, are notorious for their circuitous, often dangerous roads — a key deterrent to economic growth.

Pittsburgh's three rivers have been key commercial routes since the city's founding in 1758, and the city remains a busy inland port. The region is again looking at its rivers as an economic generator, especially at the economic prospects of pleasure boat and barge traffic. The city,

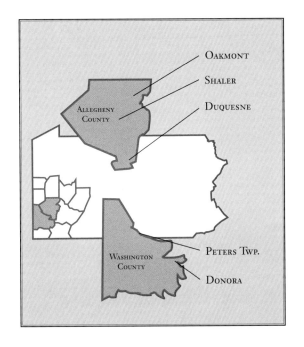

Downtown Pittsburgh, 1996
By Nina Margiotta

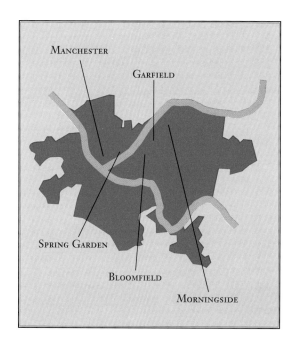

MANCHESTER

GARFIELD

SPRING GARDEN

BLOOMFIELD

MORNINGSIDE

for its part, promotes greater public access to the riverfronts by encouraging boating, parks and hiking-biking trails. Some insist that a "mixed-use" but commercial approach to riverfront development is needed, generating jobs and income as well as a higher quality of life.

Development of the riverfronts, and the use of the rivers as a cleaner, cheaper form of transportation, is gaining momentum in fits and starts. For most of the last century, Pittsburgh's rivers were viewed simply as utilitarian; riverfronts were not opportunities but contaminated, wasted pieces of land. When industry left, views of these waterfronts did not immediately change. "It was a perception problem," says Edward K. Muller, professor of history at Pitt. "During the Reagan Depression of the early '80s, Pittsburgh politicians couldn't mention reusing industrial land for something other than creating jobs. All through that decade the political viewpoint of aiding the region was in creating jobs, and that meant manufacturing jobs. It was political suicide to suggest otherwise."

There was little thought from any sector that Pittsburgh could or should take a different approach. The question was one of getting another industry to fill the crater left by steel's departure. But by the late '80s it was clear the region had more than enough reusable industrial land. People began to realize only partial, rather than total, disaster had struck, and that quality of life was crucial in attracting and maintaining the kinds of businesses Pittsburgh needed to prosper again. Still, some say it took an outsider's perspective to spark widespread realization that Pittsburgh's rivers were key to regional revitalization. Prince Charles visited the former Steel City in 1988 as part of the Remaking Cities Conference. After his inspiring words about the city's topography, especially its riverfronts, residents began to acknowledge that, for the first time in 100 years, the region's most valuable real estate was up for grabs.

The absence of development pressures on the riverfronts has allowed, to cite one example, for new waterfront townhomes, businesses, a public park, and a marina on Washington's Landing, an uninhabited island with a dramatic view of the downtown skyline. "It took time for views to change," says Muller, "but if Pittsburgh had expanded like other cities in the 1980s it would have squandered the opportunity to redevelop its riverfronts. The city still hasn't really capitalized on the opportunity. It might still miss it."

Pittsburgh's social and political culture was greatly influenced by the whims of industrial barons, the security of union jobs, and a civic-minded ethnic mix of residents living together in tightly packed communities. Most Pittsburghers did not attach great value to entrepreneurship, risk-taking, high-tech products, well-educated specialists, a flexible multi-skilled workforce, or a youth culture. (After a visit to the city in the late 1800s, Mark Twain declared that if the world ended he wanted to be in Pittsburgh, because everything happened there five years later than everywhere else.) Lagging behind the latest thing in New York or Chicago did not matter much in Pittsburgh — there was high-wage employment for residents and tax receipts for municipal and social services. The fact that the region had one of the lowest percentages of young people in the nation completing high school or going to college was not given much thought.

Today the education and health of Pittsburgh's next generation is possibly the deciding factor whether or not the city's voice will be heard in the new world order. A nurturing environment for small businesses and new people in influential positions with fresh ideas are other tools Pittsburgh needs, and does not presently have, to compete in a global economy. Fledgling endeavors that get their spark here, often at one of the area universities, too often go elsewhere to ignite. Small businesses are the fastest growing sector of the economy and the greatest generators of new jobs, but Pittsburgh ranks 25th out of the 25 largest metro areas in job creation and small business start-ups.

However, Pittsburgh has quietly developed significant high technology enterprises, such as robotics, computer software, biotechnology, environmental engineering, and health care. In the late 1980s, the National Environmental Technology Assistance Corporation chose Pittsburgh as its headquarters, attesting to the region's growing importance in that field. The Pittsburgh Technology Center continues to attract new facilities to its Monongahela River bank complex on Second Avenue. This advanced technology park thrives on a former 48-acre steel mill site. The Carnegie Mellon University/National Aeronautics and Space Administration Robotics Consortium in Lawrenceville is one of the world's leaders in technology transfer application for mobile robotics. Pittsburgh even has a World Wide Web page on the Internet. Meanwhile, Mayor Tom Murphy's vision for revitalization aims to draw large retailers as well as create an incubator atmosphere for small and medium-sized businesses in the Golden Triangle and beyond.

"People talk about what we don't have, but I'm happy that we have

USS counter-annual report

In 1981, a Tri-State Conference on Steel report questioned U.S. Steel's policy of investing in more profitable sectors of its empire, such as real estate, at the expense of its steel operations. The corporation blamed over-capacity and foreign competition, while steelworkers and their allies, such as Tri-State, predicted the destruction of many communities' economic base. Deindustrialization ultimately led to an examination of the relationship between corporations and the communities that depend upon them.

abandoned mill interior
U.S. Steel's Duquesne Works, 1988. By Lockwood Hoehl.

a cleaner city," says Bloomfield resident and realtor Orlando Scatena. "I'm not happy that people had to lose their jobs, but I'm glad Pittsburgh is a healthier, more beautiful city now. We have a new kind of pride and the transition was important. The world is changing. Our kids have different kinds of opportunities, many of them better than what they would have had years ago." People in the neighborhoods have adapted, says Scatena, who has personally seen residents open new businesses, go back to school, become truck drivers, or work in utility companies or the insurance business. Others, he says, have retired to the suburbs. "But even they still feel their place is here."

On any given day, says Scatena, clusters of older men can be seen talking on Liberty Avenue street corners. "Half of them don't live here any more but they drive in from the suburbs regularly to talk and sit on their favorite benches. They haven't lived in the neighborhood for 30 years, but if you ask them where they're from, they'll say Bloomfield. I've seen this in other neighborhoods, too. People like this city."

Harnessing the particular Pittsburgh appeal that Scatena talks about is important for the city's future, as Pittsburgh has lost 45 percent if its population since 1950. With 25 percent fewer people between the ages of 25 and 35 than other comparable regions, such as Austin, Texas, Raleigh-Durham, North Carolina, or Seattle, the overall age of Pittsburgh's "population is a concern," urban expert David Rusk told *Pittsburgh Magazine* in 1995. "It shows that you're losing a lot of your young people and a lot of your potential tax base. That definitely is not a positive sign for any city's future."

In the last decade, this 25-to-35 age group has shrunk by approximately 80,000 in six southwestern Pennsylvania counties, while the overall population has remained stagnant and the average age of residents has increased. The housing stock is also old and largely unattractive to buyers who demand sizable homes with modern conveniences. Who will live in the empty houses? How far will the city's already diminished coffers plummet and what will that mean for the basic needs and services of those left in the city?

On the other hand, the boom in some of Pittsburgh's outlying areas, to the north in Cranberry Township and to the south in Peter's Township, is a sign of economic strength. Even within the city's boundaries, many neighborhoods seem better off than a decade ago, with the Friendship area of the East End, the North Side's Mexican War Streets, and the South Side near the top of this list. Additionally, cultural institutions are emerging as development forces in Pittsburgh, with a Cultural District and riverside public park initiative downtown, the new Senator John Heinz Pittsburgh Regional History Center and a shopping complex in the Strip District, and a North Side arts and entertainment redevelopment project in the planning stages.

The city remains attractive in many ways for young people and families. It boasts numerous urban amenities (available parking comes to mind immediately), excellent health care, highly regarded schools, plenty of community activities, relatively low crime, and affordable, if old, housing. All the positives mean little, though, to families with parents and grown children who cannot find meaningful employment.

Ironically, no other region in the nation has as high a percentage of its population who live in the same place they were born. Many people leave grudgingly, and it is not uncommon to find some who return when they are looking to settle down or grow tired of the frantic pace in other cities. Pittsburgh native Carol Rubenstein moved to Philadelphia for her studies and consequently opened an art consulting business there. After nearly 10 years of success in Philadelphia, she returned to Pittsburgh in 1993 for its better quality of life and friendliness. "I still maintain an office in Philadelphia, but most of my time is spent here. I found clients here very open to broadening horizons and friendlier to work with on many levels than people that I worked with in other eastern cities." Rubenstein also finds day-to-day life in Pittsburgh more appealing. "When I first returned, I remember hurrying into a grocery line and just waiting for a battle about who got there first. Instead, the person said, 'Why don't you put your groceries in my basket so you don't have to hold them?' That's indicative of the city. It's genuinely friendly, and you can find your own niche here."

The implications of the current population distribution have affected many decisions in cultural and leadership spheres. Local businesses — restaurants, entertainments, or retail stores — tend to cater to older audiences because they are the largest core population to attract. This has raised criticism that the "same old favorites" are rehashed annually, with few contemporary or cutting-edge offerings. Concerns have emerged about patronage of cultural events, such as the Pittsburgh Symphony, once supported by individuals and corporations that are no longer here or able (or willing) to maintain past contribution levels. Reliance on the next generation to continue many of the services and assets enjoyed by Pittsburgh residents is in question, largely because of

The authors of Places Rated examined the characteristics of 329 cities. For the most part, the ranking system favored Pittsburgh for the number and variety of schools in the region; the existence of numerous cultural amenities, largely the product of industrial philanthropy; the number of hospital beds; a low crime rate; a temperate climate; and the proximity of recreational areas in the Tri-state region. A little detail on the rankings:

Education — 7th
Arts — 12th
Health care — 14th
Transportation — 76th
Crime — 78th
Climate — 87th
Recreation — 90th
Economics — 185th

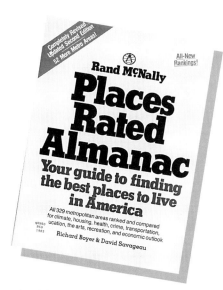

"Most livable city"

In 1985, the Places Rated Almanac listed Pittsburgh as the
nation's "Most Livable City." Many Pittsburghers – and
most of America – seemed surprised, especially after the
loss of industrial jobs and nearly half of the city's
population since 1950. Others responded with celebrations
and good-humored boosterism, savoring the much-needed
respite from gloomy reports about the city.

the striking out-migration of young people and increasing competition
for the dollars of those left.

For similar demographic reasons, Pittsburgh's leadership remains
overwhelmingly homogeneous. Understandably, many area leaders do
not have a background in how to encourage economic development not
geared to a middle-age or older (and primarily white) population. That
means the city is largely reliant on a few influential institutions and
individuals of like mind. Recent city and county elections suggest this is
changing, with longstanding incumbents being voted out in place of
new blood. Some corporate and civic boards of directors are making
efforts to engage and include younger Pittsburgh residents among their
number, and some members of the foundation community have invested
in forward-thinking endeavors, such as the Heinz Endowment's current
involvement in the city's Environmental Initiative.

Change may be coming, but it is in no hurry. Civic structures for
economic development have so far failed to produce significant results.
Robert Mehrabian, president of Carnegie Mellon University, believes
centralizing the effort would help (and responsive noises were heard in
the organizational machinery in late 1995). "More than 200 private and
public organizations are involved in economic development activities
without effective coordination and focused, data-based, strategic
actions," he notes in the preface to the Allegheny Conference's 1993
study of regional economic development. Mehrabian found a disjointed
vision of the future, growing polarization, and overlapping institutional
agendas that did little but create rivals for limited resources.

It sometimes seems that the city's 700-plus bridges, connecting
Pittsburgh's disparate neighborhoods like stitches from a giant needle,
are the only things that hold the place together. Rifts and feuds are as
endemic as mountains and valleys. From neighborhoods with three community groups all purporting to do the same work but refusing to talk to
one another, to a county with 133 municipalities and 43 school districts
that take largely the same attitude on a regional scale, southwestern
Pennsylvania may be the most fractious region in the nation. It is this
fragmentation that many civic leaders say must be addressed for the
region to move forward. Recent strategic plans put forth by the
Allegheny Conference suggest there is no lack of high-caliber ideas in
Pittsburgh, but rather that the absence of coordinated leadership is one
of the greatest liabilities.

Urbanologist Rusk's answer to this problem, echoed by a number of

public and private leaders, is a strong central county government, mirroring the recent regionalization of cities such as Charlotte, Indianapolis, and Jacksonville, Florida. The problem, say a number of regional officials, is that Pennsylvania state law all but prohibits such initiatives.

If History Can Be Trusted

What Pittsburgh may be experiencing is its coming of age as a true American city. It may be wrestling with growing pains, and finding out some things that it just did not want to know. Pittsburgh is not the innocent it once was. While still one of the least crime-ridden metro areas of its size, the emergence of national plagues — youth gangs, the high cost of traditional public and civic services, damage wrought by suburbanization, guns in schools, an increasing racial divide — are all evident. Residents who grew up believing urban ills and bizarre crimes reflect a systemic breakdown that happens to other people in other places find these changes hard to accept. This insular view manages to isolate the city more than repel any real or imagined outside threats.

At the same time, looking inward has produced a tenacious sense of "taking care of our own" and has greatly aided in maintaining the city's unique integrity, especially its many distinct neighborhoods. Residents from Morningside to Spring Garden to the South Side slopes recount anecdotes about the underground economies and plain

Bradshaw/Stargell

Two of Pittsburgh's three professional sports teams won championships in 1979. Willie Stargell of the Pirates and the Steelers' Terry Bradshaw (sparkling white socks) posed as Sports Illustrated's "Sportsmen of the Year" with some real steelers at the Jones and Laughlin mill in Pittsburgh. The Steelers won three Super Bowl crowns in the 1970s. Renewing the proud tradition of sports excellence elevated the spirits of many Pittsburghers at a time of crippling economic uncertainty.

"The '79 sports season made it official. Howard Cosell made it official. And network TV told the world: Pittsburgh is the City of Champions. The Black and Gold finally changed the city's nickname from Steel City."

— *Pittsburgh: City of Champions (1980)*

Heat hood (right)
Worn in the 1990s at "ET," it is similar to the type worn in the photograph below, except that it is made from a non-asbestos fabric.

Blast furnace, man in heat suit (below)
At the Edgar Thomson Works in Braddock in 1980, a worker retrieves a sample of molten steel for chemical analysis. Aluminized heat suits are still worn by steelworkers who labor around hot liquid metal. In modern steel mills, modernization has not completely eliminated the need for skilled workers.

"Save Dorothy"

Named for the wife of former U.S. Steel president Leslie B. Worthington, the Dorothy Six blast furnace at the Duquesne Works became a symbol of steel's demise. U.S. Steel had built the furnace, the largest in the world, in the early 1960s, only to shut it down 25 years later. To many, the furnace symbolized the vacillating commitment of domestic steel makers in a highly competitive modern era. To others, Dorothy Six promised a future, largely unrealized, in which viable facilities might be saved and operated as employee-owned ventures. USX toppled the giant furnace in the summer of 1988.

Homestead / river (below)

by Charlee Brodsky

U.S. Steel's Homestead Works fell silent in 1986. The mill, known internationally for the violent strike of 1892, deserved greater fame for the amount of steel its workers turned out after a massive expansion during World War II. By the 1980s, mill closings in the valley had diminished traffic on the Monongahela. Although the Homestead High Level Bridge was showing its age (1987), the river appears serene and timeless, seemingly untouched by all that humans had done here.

Kids in window/Homestead, 1989
by Charlee Brodsky

Homestead row homes, 1989
by Charlee Brodsky

Overleaf
Braddock, 1989
by Charlee Brodsky

old spunk that emerges in Pittsburgh during hard times. In the years right after mill closings in the mid-'80s idled 7,000 people in Lawrenceville alone, up to 20 percent of that neighborhood's economy took the form of bartering, says Lois Garcia, a long-time community organizer. "Someone would fix your car and you would cut their hair, or baby-sit, or someone would lend you their truck while someone else ran grocery errands," she says. "This wasn't an occasional favor, this was an entire underground economy based on people helping people." While many Lawrenceville residents have retrained, found work, or retired since the mills closed, the sense of neighborliness persists today, as it does elsewhere in Pittsburgh. City assistance has made its impact, too, through small grants and low-interest mortgages for homeowners and businesses. "The neighborhood should have died," says Garcia. "The government people who came here to do surveys said so. Their reports say it should have been down to the ground, but the people hung on. The people here are really doers."

When you are living it, 20 years can be an eternity, but historically it is a millisecond. Pittsburgh has entered the second decade of the most severe manufacturing decline faced by any major metropolitan region in the country. Similarly severe economic downturns dogged the city during two notable decades of the 19th century, but the Pittsburgh economy did rebound. In the 1870s, severe recessions leading to the worst labor unrest in U.S. history gave way to the 1880s, when steel brought Pittsburgh global fame as the wonder of the Industrial Age. Tremendous gloom and layoffs by the thousands returned in the early 1890s, before an accumulation of riches so fantastic in the first decade of the 20th century made Pittsburgh, some have calculated, the richest city the world has ever known. Old-timers today also remember their hometown after the Great Depression of the 1930s, which hit few urban centers as hard as it hit Pittsburgh. Yet the calamities of the '30s stimulated the forces of postwar private-public partnerships which, by the 1950s, made Pittsburgh the envy of far larger cities in far newer parts of the nation.

In 1989, the eloquent urban portraitist Brendan Gill of *New Yorker* magazine called Pittsburgh an inimitable American presence, suggesting that if any city could bounce back from hard times, it is Pittsburgh. More time still may be needed for a new generation of cooperative thinkers to evolve who can sort out a new generation of obstacles and opportunities. But looking at the past, there is cause to think that Pittsburgh has history on its side.

Illustration Credits

CHAPTER 1, *A Contested Land*

PAGE

xiii — Courtesy of Cranbrook Institute of Science, Detroit

2 — Top, Historical Society of Western Pennsylvania Museum, Gift of Helen Savage, (photograph by Chisholm Photographic); bottom, HSWP Museum, Gift of Lawrence M. Anderson

3 — Courtesy of Newberry Library, Chicago

4 — HSWP Museum, Gift of William Mowry (Chisholm Photographic)

5 — HSWP Museum, Gift of Mary L. Stevenson (Chisholm Photographic)

6 — Top, HSWP Library & Archives, Gift of Julia Morgan Harding (photo by Connie Karaffa); below, HSWP Museum, Gift of Charles A. McClintock (photo by Matt Bulvony)

7 — Top, HSWP Museum, Gift of Julia Morgan Harding (Matt Bulvony); center, HSWP L&A

8 — Courtesy of Washington & Jefferson College Historical Collection, Washington, Pa.

9 — HSWP Museum, Bequest of Elizabeth Hornek Gordon (Matt Bulvony)

10 — Top photograph by Chisholm Photographic; bottom courtesy of Philadelphia Museum of Art. HSWP Museum purchase, funds provided by Mrs. Thomas Lewis.

11 — Top, HSWP Museum purchase (Chisholm Photographic); bottom, HSWP Museum, Gift of Mrs. and Mrs. S. Harris Johnson (Connie Karaffa)

12 — Top, HSWP Museum, Gift of Henry K. Siebeneck (Chisholm Photographic); bottom, HSWP Museum, Gift of Mrs. William A. Seifert (Chisholm Photographic)

13 — HSWP Museum, Gift of Henry K. Siebeneck (Matt Bulvony)

CHAPTER 2, *City on the Move*

PAGE

14-15 — Historical Society of Western Pennsylvania Museum (photograph by Chisholm Photographic)

16 — Top, HSWP Museum, Gift of Emma Zug (Chisholm Photographic); bottom, courtesy of Ohio Historical Society, Columbus

19, 20 — HSWP Museum, Gift of Benjamin Thaw (Chisholm Photographic)

22 — HSWP Museum purchase (Chisholm Photographic)

23 — HSWP Museum, Gift of Col. Edward J. Allen (Chisholm Photographic)

24 — Top, HSWP Museum, Bequest of Elizabeth W. Firuski; center, HSWP Museum purchase — Brendel Fund (Chisholm Photographic); bottom, HSWP Museum, Gift of the Pittsburgh Chapter, Early American Glass Club (Chisholm Photographic)

25 — HSWP Library & Archives, Gift of Benjamin Thaw, Mary Thaw Thompson & Mary Thaw Barnes

26 — HSWP L&A

27 — Top, HSWP Museum (Chisholm Photographic); center, HSWP Museum, Gift of Charles W. Prine, Jr. (photo by Matt Bulvony); HSWP Museum (Chisholm Photographic)

28 — Top, HSWP Museum, Gift of Mrs. Earle E. Ewing (photo by Matt Bulvony); left center, HSWP Museum, Gift of Mr. and Mrs. James H. Beal (Chisholm Photographic); right center, HSWP Museum, Gift of Columbia Gas of Pennsylvania (Chisholm Photographic); bottom, HSWP Museum, Gift of Joseph A. Borkowski (Chisholm Photographic)

29 — HSWP L&A Map Collection

31 — HSWP L&A, Lyon, Shorb Collection

CHAPTER 3, *The Industrial City*

PAGE

32-33 — Collection of the Westmoreland Museum of Art

34 — Historical Society of Western Pennsylvania Library & Archives

36 — HSWP Museum, Gift of Mr. and Mrs. Edward Garba (photograph by Chisholm Photographic)

37 — HSWP Museum, Gift of Robert J. Trombetta

39 — Courtesy of Univ. of Pittsburgh, Archives of Industrial Society

40 — HSWP Museum (Chisholm Photographic)

41 — From Margaret F. Byington, *Homestead: Households of a Mill Town*

42-43 — HSWP L&A Postcard Collection

44 — HSWP L&A, Gift of Amelia Zeller

45 — Top, Courtesy of Johnstown Area Heritage Association, Gift of the Burdnak and Koval families

46 — HSWP L&A, Gift of Michael J. Haraburda

47 — HSWP L&A, Gift of Percy Mills

48 — Top, HSWP L&A, Gift of Anna M. Toth; inset, HSWP Museum, Gift of Erma Balogh (Chisholm Photographic)

49 — Top, HSWP L&A, Gift of Anna M. Toth; bottom, courtesy of Patchwork Voices Project, Penn State-Fayette Campus

50, 51 — HSWP L&A, Gift of Anna M. Toth

52 — Top, from David Demarest, et. al., *The River Ran Red* (used by persmission); bottom, HSWP L&A, Gift of Lee Cecchini

53 — Top, HSWP Museum, Gift of Mrs. Lawrence Litchfield; middle, HSWP Museum (Chisholm Photographic)

54-55 — Courtesy of Mrs. H.J. Heinz III

56 — Top left: HSWP L&A, Gift of Margaret Barr; inset, HSWP Museum (Chisholm Photographic); top right, HSWP Museum (Chisholm Photographic); HSWP L&A, Gift of LTV Corp.

57   Top, HSWP Museum, Gift of Pittsburgh History & Landmarks Foundation (left), and (right), HSWP Museum, Gift of Nancy Ann Brandon (Chisholm Photographic)

58   Top, HSWP L&A, Postcard Collection; bottom, courtesy of Hunt Library, Carnegie Mellon Univ.

59   Hunt Library, Carnegie Mellon Univ.

60   Top left, HSWP L&A, Gift of Sarah and Rachel McClelland; top right, Gift of Rosemary H. Meyerjack; bottom, Courtesy of Kaufmann's, a division of the May Department Stores Co.

61   HSWP L&A, Gift of Thomas M. Galley

CHAPTER 4, *The Hill: A City Neighborhood*

PAGE

62-3   Historical Society of Western Pennsylvania Library & Archives, Gift of Sidney Teller

64   Courtesy of Carnegie Library of Pittsburgh

67   *Pittsburgh Courier*, June 16, 1923

68   HSWP L&A, Gift of Sidney Teller

70   Pittsburgh Courier Photographic Archives

71   HSWP L&A

72   Univ. of Pittsburgh, Archives of Industrial Society

73   HSWP L&A, Gift of Mrs. Ida Mae Jefferson

74   Top, HSWP L&A, Gift of the Antonucci family; bottom, HSWP Museum (photograph by Chisholm Photographic)

75   Top, HSWP L&A, Gift of Agnes M. Samreny; lower, Gift of St. Benedict the Moor Church

76   Top, HSWP L&A, Gift of Sidney Teller; bottom, HSWP L&A

77   Top, HSWP L&A, Gift of Sidney Teller; bottom, HSWP Museum, Gift of Thelma West (Chisholm Photographic)

78   Courtesy of the National Archives

79   Left, HSWP Museum, Gift of Michael Haraburda (Chisholm Photographic); top right, courtesy of Florence Leebov; bottom, Pittsburgh Courier Photographic Library

80   Top, HSWP L&A, Gift of Frank Bolden; bottom, Pittsburgh Courier Photographic Library

81   Top left, HSWP L&A, Gift of Sidney Santman; right, Gift of Olga Krasofsky; middle, Gift of the Trustees and Congregation Bethel A.M.E. Church; bottom, HSWP Museum, Gift of Sidney Santman

82   Original in color. Collection of the Westmoreland Museum of Art

83   HSWP L&A, Gift of Vicki Battles

CHAPTER 5, *Moving to the Suburbs*

PAGE

85   Courtesy of Standard Oil of New Jersey Collection, Photographic Archives, Univ. of Louisville

86   *Pittsburgh Press*

89   Historical Society of Western Pennsylvania Library & Archives Postcard Collection

90   Courtesy of the National Archives

91   HSWP Museum

92   Model miniature lent by Dr. Richard Bannon (photograph by Chisholm Photographic); brochure courtesy of Ira Gordon.

94   Broadsides HSWP L&A; photograph courtesy of National Museum of American History

95   Top, HSWP L&A, Gift of Marie Hredzak; bottom courtesy of George and Loretto Gatto

96   Painting HSWP Museum (Chisholm Photographic); top, courtesy of Carnegie Library of Pittsburgh; bottom, courtesy of *Pittsburgh Post-Gazette*

97   Refrigerator HSWP Museum (Chisholm Photographic); ad from *American Home* magazine.

98   Top, courtesy of Kennywood Park; sign HSWP Museum Collection (Chisholm Photographic); bottom, courtesy of Eat'n Park Corp.

99   Courtesy of Univ. of Pittsburgh, Archives of Industrial Society

CHAPTER 6, *After the Renaissance*

PAGE

100   Collection of the Westmoreland Museum of Art, Gift of Mrs. Alvin M. Owsley

101   Historical Society of Western Pennsylvnia Library and Archives, Gift of Allegheny Conference on Community Development

105   Top, HSWP L&A, Gift of Allegheny Conference; bottom, courtesy of National Archives

106   Top, HSWP L&A, Gift of Allegheny Conference; bottom, HSWP Museum (photograph by Chisholm Photographic)

107   HSWP L&A, Gift of Allegheny Conference

108   HSWP Museum

112   HSWP L&A, Gift of Charlie McCollester

113   HSWP L&A

115   HSWP L&A

116   *Sports Illustrated*/Time Inc.

117   Top, HSWP Museum (Chisholm Photographic); bottom, courtesy of *Pittsburgh Post-Gazette*

118   Top, HSWP L&A; t-shirt HSWP Museum

A Note on this Book

This book was set in Janson and Futura typefaces on recycled, acid-free paper.

Printed by Geyer Printing Company, Inc., in Pittsburgh.

Preparation of the color illustrations by Page Imaging, Inc., of Pittsburgh.

Smythe sewn binding by Pittsburgh Binding.

Design by Ron Donoughe.